"There is so much I can say about this fantastic, necessary, radical, beautiful, powerful book, but the main thing I want to say (well, actually, I kind of want to SHOUT it) is THANK YOU, VIRGIE! THANK YOU! Thank you for envisioning and writing a book like this, that I can give to my daughter, and every young woman I encounter. Would it be weird if I stood on the street and just handed out copies?!"

> —**Kate Schatz**, *New York Times* bestselling author of the *Rad Women* series, including *Rad American Women A-Z* and *Rad Women Worldwide*

"*Every body exists the exact way it's meant to exist.* While this shouldn't be a radical concept, it absolutely is. This is the book I wish I'd read when I was 14. Reading it now feels like a healing for my teenage self. The wisdom in this book is absolutely necessary for the critical paradigm shift needed to liberate young women from the toxicity of our current cultural norms. Tovar is a wealth of vibrant stories and radical insight. Armed with her tiny cactus and gigantic umbrella, she joyously jiggles a pathway to freedom and self-acceptance, illuminating the first steps for each of us to make our own individual journeys."

> —**Reagan Jackson**, program director for Young Women Empowered, award-winning journalist, and prod̴   and cohost of the *Deep End Podcast*

"Virgie Tovar has penned the instruction and empowerment guide that young women not only need, but deserve. With its direct guidance and relatable stories, the irresistible beauty and profound power of *The Self-Love Revolution* is that it is equal parts love letter, action guide, permission granter, and manifesto. An impassioned and insightful treatise, it inspires its readers to critically question our cultural beauty standards, and passionately commit to demanding something better for themselves and the world. This is the rare book that can change not just hearts and minds, but also our culture."

—**Rosie Molinary, MFA**, author of *Beautiful You* and *Hijas Americanas*

"How I wish I'd had this book in my arsenal as a fat Colombian girl growing up in the very white, mostly thin suburbs of New Jersey. I cannot wait to share it with my own daughters as they grow older. It will be an antidote to the toxic messaging on beauty standards, dieting, race, and wellness they will no doubt come into contact with. I cannot wait to share it with everyone, TBH—with those who have never heard of radical body positivity or fat acceptance before, with seasoned activists, with everyone."

—**Marie Southard Ospina, MA**, writer, editor, and fat acceptance advocate

"Virgie Tovar is the badass bestie we all prayed for in middle school. Her new book is a revolutionary manifesto, one that's essential reading not just for surviving the most toxic parts of modern culture, but also for embracing our own needs and power. Unflinchingly real—with page after page of quote-worthy truth bombs— this book is a delicious call to arms for the next generation of girl rebels."

—**Laurie Santos**, professor of psychology at Yale University, and host of *The Happiness Lab* podcast

"This book *does* have the power to start a revolution! Virgie tells the *truth*—all the truths—girls of color need to know about their bodies and their own worth, from history, to systemic oppression, to her own instructive story. Virgie brings girls a profound message that is totally accessible, never patronizing. She is a brilliant writer and thinker in body positivity, and she transmits to teen girls of color what grown women learn from her every day. There are other body positivity books out there, but this is *the one* the girls of color I work with truly need."

—**Jennifer Berger**, body image educator; and executive director of the nonprofit organization, About-Face

the *instant* help solutions series

Young people today need mental health resources more than ever. That's why New Harbinger created the **Instant Help Solutions Series** especially for teens. Written by leading psychologists, physicians, and professionals, these evidence-based self-help books offer practical tips and strategies for dealing with a variety of mental health issues and life challenges teens face, such as depression, anxiety, bullying, eating disorders, trauma, and self-esteem problems.

Studies have shown that young people who learn healthy coping skills early on are better able to navigate problems later in life. Engaging and easy-to-use, these books provide teens with the tools they need to thrive—at home, at school, and on into adulthood.

This series is part of the **New Harbinger Instant Help Books** imprint, founded by renowned child psychologist Lawrence Shapiro. For a complete list of books in this series, visit newharbinger.com.

THE *SELF-LOVE* REVOLUTION

Radical Body Positivity for Girls of Color

VIRGIE TOVAR, MA

Instant Help Books

An Imprint of New Harbinger Publications, Inc.

Publisher's Note

Distributed in Canada by Raincoast Books

Copyright © 2020 by Virgie Tovar
Instant Help Books
An imprint of New Harbinger Publications, Inc.
5674 Shattuck Avenue
Oakland, CA 94609
www.newharbinger.com

Cover design by Amy Shoup/Sara Christian

Acquired by Jennye Garibaldi

Edited by Teja Watson

All Rights Reserved

33614082354746

Library of Congress Cataloging-in-Publication Data on file

Printed in the United States of America

22   21   20

10   9   8   7   6   5   4   3   2   1   First Printing

For every girl who has felt ugly, wrong, bad, weak—
you are beautiful, you are right, you are good,
you are powerful beyond imagination.

Contents

Part Three Be You, Not What Someone Else Thinks You Should Be

Introduction

Dear Person Reading This,

Hello.

There's a myth that girls don't understand their bodies and that you can't trust your body. The truth is that you know your body better than anyone on this planet ever will. This makes you an expert. Your body tells you when it likes something and when it doesn't. Your body tells you when it likes a person and when it doesn't. Your body knows when you're in danger and when you're safe.

Listen to your body. It's giving you information all the time. Your job is to clear away as many obstacles as you possibly can so that you can hear all the messages and secrets it has for you. Obstacles include things like toxic relationships, abusive households, teachers who put you down, friends who don't support you, bullying and emotional abuse, self-criticism, dieting, sexism, and fatphobia.

Girls grow up learning to be afraid of their bodies because other people teach them to feel that way. Your body is political because when you listen to it, you have the power to radically transform the culture, the planet, and history. Of course the culture is telling you not to listen to your body, because if you do that means that the culture isn't in control of you—you are!

This can feel super scary. It's also totally awesome, and absolutely necessary if you're going to have the sparkly life you totally deserve to have.

Whenever you're at a crossroads, just ask yourself two questions: "Does my body deep down like this?" and "Does this honor the magical babe that I am?" And if the answer to both is yes, do that thing.

In addition to being a book about your relationship to your body, this is also a book about body justice.

I think of body justice like it's a three-story house. The *first* floor is very important because this is the floor that's about your relationship to yourself and your body; this is the floor dedicated to self-love. Self-love can be defined lots of ways, but for now let's say it's about recognizing that perfection is not something we need to earn, but instead is a natural state that we already *always* possess.

The *second* floor of the house is about your community. This floor is about sharing with our friends and the people we love tools and education that will help them live their best lives.

The *third* floor is about the culture, and changing it so that everyone can feel safe in the body they have. Changing the culture can start with imagining what we want to see in the future.

In this book we'll talk about all three of these floors—the whole house.

But first, let me tell you who's writing this thing you're reading.

My name is Virgie. I'm thirty-six years old. I was born and raised in California, in the Bay Area. I'm a Taurus. My mother is Mexican-American and my dad is from Iran. I was raised by my grandparents, both Mexican immigrants. I'm kind of a hippie bohemian who lives by the ocean in San Francisco. I believe in magic. I believe in the power of doughnuts. I am a fat activist, meaning I fight against fat hatred in our culture so that people of all sizes can live good lives (not just thin people). I weigh 250 pounds. I have a bachelor's degree and a master's degree. I love coffee, traveling to other countries, Chihuahuas, and neon nail polish. I have friends all over the world; most of them are rad women. I identify as a feminist, an anti-racist, and a proud fat babe. The things that matter to me most are: social justice, my friends, eating delicious stuff, seeing as much of the world as possible, healing myself from a dysfunctional childhood and years of hating myself for being fat, dating people I really like, and wearing the biggest jewelry I can find.

Radical body positivity starts with getting to know yourself: who you are, what you like, and what you want. One of the ways I've gotten to know myself is through writing—especially in my journal. There will be lots of opportunities to journal throughout this book; at the end of each chapter there will be journal prompts. You can use a journal you already have, buy a new one, or make your own with paper you bind with staples, ribbon, or twine.

Maybe the answers to these questions could be your first entry.

write About It

Start with your name and age; then write about where you were born and raised. What's your astrological sign? Write down three things you love. Write about the things that matter most to you right now. End with some changes you want to see in the world.

Before we start revolutionizing anything, I have to tell you something.

It took me a long time to start this book. Like, a really, really long time. Sometimes writers say things like that when they mean that they've been working on a book for ten years—say, their memoir. That makes sense, because writing about yourself is complicated, and it's a vulnerable act to share private things about your life, knowing that anyone can read it while you're still walking around on the planet.

But I'm not talking about that kind of situation. I'm talking about avoidance, procrastination, and actual terror.

I avoided it like a pro. I read books about people who cared about this topic. I interviewed girls and young women of color. I interviewed people who work with girls and young women of color. I journaled about it. I pulled tarot cards for it. I'd drink coffee and doodle ideas about what the book could look like. I talked to my friends for hours about how I should do it.

I took a Greyhound bus for seven hours from San Francisco to Reno, Nevada (where my friend had offered to put me up for a few days so I could write without any distractions). I lost my diary on the bus and panicked that everyone at the Greyhound company would take turns reading it in a fake voice and tweeting all of it—page by page—over a series of months, and tagging me.

I started taking weird, conceptual selfies in alleys that had murals in them. Front-facing. Then some with my back to the camera. Then some where I was looking back at the camera over my shoulder while not smiling.

At one point I was walking around the aisles of a Michaels craft store, shopping for pom-poms I was going to turn into bomb earrings—which I did—while processing by phone with my friend Mel in Indiana for two hours about how I was going to make this book *perfect.*

And then something weird happened. I forced myself to sit down and write this out—to just be honest about how hard this was for me. And right then a thunderstorm started. Literally. Lightning. Rain. Car alarms going off. Trees getting tossed around. Like some Armageddon-type ancestral sign from the cosmos beyond, Girl.

Inspired by these powerful bolts of mysterious electricity, I came to a realization. It was ironic that I was trying to write about body justice while putting so much pressure on myself to create something flawless. The truth is, this book won't be perfect. You'll think of better ways to express what I'm trying to say. You'll think of better activities. Despite my best intentions, you might even feel like there are moments when I missed the point or said something offensive.

That's what it means to be a human. That's what it means to show up. Not to strive for perfection, but to know that everything we could ever need lives inside us. It means recognizing that sacred gift in every person, no matter what their body looks like, no matter what it can do, no matter their gender, no matter how much money they do or don't have, no matter how they get down, no matter whom they love or desire, and no matter how they talk about what God is.

I'm not trying to say that we need to turn the other cheek or love our enemy or anything like that. I don't believe in turning the other cheek in the face of injustice or pretending to love someone who treats people like they're garbage. It's important to protect ourselves from people and institutions that seek to harm us. And I'll talk more about that in this book.

What I'm trying to say is that you have the power to transform stuff that isn't perfect, stuff that sucks, into something meaningful for you. And you have the power to look past what society teaches us about ourselves and others, and intentionally create a beautiful relationship with yourself and with the people who lift you up.

I brought out my tarot deck the night before I wrote what you're reading right now, and I pulled The Star, a card that is all about being yourself, learning to let go of what has hurt you in the past and to embrace who you are becoming—honoring who you are meant to be.

In my deck, The Star card has David Bowie on it.

Bowie was a musical genius who wore amazing outfits. He was a chameleon who was constantly shape-shifting into different personas. He was always true to himself, and NEVER let other people's ideas of what a man should look like, act like, or sing like get in his way. Some people thought he was psychic. He had this incredible voice and his eyes were different colors. There was a lightning bolt on his forehead in the card. I feel like David Bowie and this electrical storm that started after I sat down to start this book are good signs that if you're reading this book you are meant to.

This book might change the way you see, the way you think, the way you talk, the way you look in the mirror, the way you touch your skin, the way you deal with cruel people, the way you see others, and the way you see yourself. Be open. Be critical. If you need to cry, do it. If you need to get mad, do it. If you feel sad, feel it. If you feel called to action, move on that feeling. If you feel like you need to put this aside for a while (even if it's a long while), that's okay. Read the chapters you're most excited about first. Save the others for later.

This book is a link between you and me, between you and history, between you and thousands of years of injustice that worked very hard to keep you from the knowledge of your own power.

I believe that oppression doesn't have to be a part of our lives, but we have to fight really hard to get what we deserve in this culture, and sometimes we still don't get it. That's not fair. That's how things are right now, but maybe they won't always be that way. Don't believe anyone who tells you unfairness is natural or normal. They're lying. You have the right to dream of something better. You have the right to demand it.

I am here to tell you: You are powerful beyond belief. I think, after that electrical storm, I realized that my only real job is to tell you that, to convince you of that, in two hundred pages or less.

> You are powerful beyond belief.

You ready?

XO,

Virgie

Part one

OUR MESSY WORLD

1

Nine Points That Explode Beauty Standards

Here's something that always surprises people: we learn who is (and isn't) beautiful from the culture.

We're not born believing that one kind of hair or skin color or one kind of body is more appealing than others. We learn that as we grow up. How do we learn that? The same way we learn everything else: through other people's behavior, TV, the fashion world, books, the internet, advertising, magazines, who we see playing heroes and villains in movies, the mannequins at the mall, the things our friends and family say, bullies, and the other people around us.

Just like people who grow up in Boston have a different accent from people who grow up in Dallas, our understanding of who and what is beautiful changes a little depending on where we live.

For the past ten years I have lived in San Francisco, a rich city with a population that's almost half white. Here, athletic, slender people are considered the most beautiful (which is common in wealthy places). I grew up, though, in a mostly brown city where I learned two different ideas of beauty: thin was considered attractive, but so was being "thick." "Thick" meant you were bigger in the "right" places—like your hips, chest, and butt—but you had a small waist and flat stomach. Like most girls, I didn't meet either of those ideas of beauty and I felt like it was my fault.

Today I know that the beauty ideals I learned were totally busted, and that I can redefine who and what I think of as beautiful. Nowadays, I think fat is beautiful. I think dark curly hair is beautiful. I think my friend Andrea, who has one hand instead of two, and my friend Amber, who has legs of different lengths, are beautiful.

Let's back up a little and ask an important question: What is beauty?

I think most humans would agree that a sunset is beautiful, a beach is beautiful, and a mountain is beautiful. However, when it comes to most other things, the answer to that question is, "It depends." It depends on who you ask, when you ask, and where you ask. If you asked someone in China in the year 1177, they might tell you that very tiny feet that are just a few inches long are beautiful. If you asked someone in Northern Thailand in the year 1993, they might tell you that very long, giraffe-like necks are beautiful. If you asked someone in the United States in the year 2020, they might tell you that light eyes and very thin bodies are beautiful.

Beauty is an idea. It's an idea that impacts mostly women and girls.

What is a beauty standard or a beauty ideal? It's the physical qualities that women and girls feel pressured to achieve and maintain.

Even though beauty standards have a huge impact on our lives, they are *not* something we are born understanding, as I said before.

We learn what is beautiful from the people and media around us. We learn who is beautiful from the culture we are born into.

The nine points I'm about to share with you will help you as you move forward in reading this book. I'll be talking about them more than once, and they are an important foundation for critically examining—or questioning—how we understand our bodies. Questioning what we've been taught about ourselves is the first step to getting into an LTR (long-term relationship) with radical body positivity.

1. The idea of beauty changes from place to place and over time

Among the Kayans of Northern Thailand and Burma, a very long neck is considered beautiful for girls and women. So from a very young age, while their bones and muscles are still forming, young girls have metal rings put around their necks by older women. They keep adding rings until their necks are two or three times longer than the average human neck. Even though the rings can lead to bruising and rib compression, a long neck is a prized sign of feminine beauty.

In China from the tenth to the twentieth century, tiny feet were in fashion. So foot-binding was a common practice among Chinese girls, typically beginning between ages four and six. The size of a child's foot was considered the ideal size for a grown woman. Parents would break and remold their girls' feet, wrapping bandages tightly around them so they would look like hooves. The girls couldn't walk, but this made girls more eligible for marriage. Only very poor people didn't bind, because they couldn't afford the loss of the ability to walk.

In parts of Mauritania and Niger today, girls and young women who are fat are more likely to get married.[1] The men in these areas love fat women. Stretch marks on the upper arms are considered a super-beautiful, enviable trait. The older women in these societies are paid to force-feed the younger girls very rich food, and the girls get punished if they don't eat all they are told to eat. Sometimes girls eat weight-gaining medicine that was designed for animals, and some of them die from it.

I have one final example of a beauty standard. In another part of the world, girls and young women are pressured to be as thin as possible. It starts when they are very young. Often by five years old they have already been introduced to something called "fatphobia," which is a form of discrimination that says that fatness is bad and ugly and that thinness is good and attractive. Sometimes girls and women go on things called "diets" for ten, twenty, thirty, forty, or fifty years—during which they restrict how much they eat and go to places called "gyms," where they engage in physical activity that is meant to change their shape into something more socially acceptable. They learn that some foods are "good" and some foods are "evil." Even though science has indicated clearly that these diets ultimately do not work, girls and women still engage in this behavior in order to be accepted. They often lose and gain the same pounds over decades, dedicating thousands of dollars and hours to this process, and report that it makes them feel like they are improving themselves.

Any guesses where the fourth place is? If you said the United States, you're correct.

I have a friend who's a sociologist, and she says that the job of a sociologist is to turn things that feel familiar into things that feel strange. Imagine explaining to someone who has never visited the planet what beauty looks like where you live.

2. In the United States (and many other places), racism shapes what is considered beautiful

If you're like me, you were taught to think that light skin, light eyes, and light hair are the most beautiful. It's not an accident that in the United States, this is what is considered beautiful. The idea that white features—including light eyes and skin, straight hair, and bodies shaped like Northern Europeans'—are a sign of beauty comes from racist notions that white people are superior.

In part, the current idea of beauty in the US began when the first Spanish and British settlers landed on our shores about four hundred years ago. With them came slavery and the ideas of property owner-ship and expanding settlements to take up more land. A small group of rich white dudes decided to steal a bunch of land to ensure that they and their families would be rich and powerful. They cleared the land they wanted to take by killing native populations, and they built and maintained the land they'd stolen by enslaving Africans. They justified this by saying that the native and African people they were exploiting were inferior.

At the very end of the 1600s, these settlers invented the idea of whiteness,. In 1682, the word "white" appears for the first time in a Virginia law that outlawed marriage between black and white people. They argued that white people were naturally more intelligent than everyone else. The belief of white superiority extended to ideas of who was and wasn't attractive.

Even though it's been a really long time since then, our country has done little to truly make things right. Just like people, when a country doesn't recognize when it's done something wrong and then apologize and try to right its wrongs, it can't heal. The open wound of that wrongdoing lives on to this day in the form of racism. Racism still exists, and so do racist beauty ideals. Since the United States makes a lot of movies and other media that are watched all over the world, more and more, the beauty ideal here is becoming the beauty ideal everywhere.

The idea that lighter features are more beautiful stems from the idea that dark people are inferior and common, while lighter people are superior and rare. We have been taught to see things like straight hair and light eyes as better, but the truth is that all hair types, all skin colors, all body shapes and sizes, and all eye colors are equally awesome.

3. "Beauty" is an idea that is totally imaginary (and that means you can make up your own idea)

Okay, so beauty is a thing called a "social construction." That's a fancy way of saying it's make-believe—but it's a powerful example of make-believe, because so many people have bought into it. When we break down the phrase "social construction," we get two components: "social," which refers to society or culture, and "construction," which refers to something that is created. In short, beauty is an idea that is created by society. Because it's an idea, we can break it down and change it.

4. When we dedicate a lot of time to the pursuit of beauty, we lose time we could be spending doing other stuff that may be more important to us

What matters to you the most? What are you interested in? What is a dream of yours? There are about one million things that humans are capable of doing that we haven't even thought of yet. Here are some things I had time for once I stopped obsessing over how pretty other people thought I was: making my own pom-pom earrings, drawing weird and excellent moments in my journal with my glitter crayons, taking baths, altering clothes, learning how to write Spanish better, writing cards to my friends, learning how to find herbs out in nature, drinking tea, making blackberry muffins, writing books, making zines, trying new coffee, reading articles by smart people, going to political organizing meetings, and talking to my tiny cactus Lumpy about my problems. If you decided to stop doing one beauty practice you don't like that much, what might you do instead?

5. The beauty industry relies upon women and girls feeling insecure and afraid

Guess what? It's really hard to get people to spend a bunch of money all the time unless they feel like the stuff they're buying is going to give them something they don't already have. We live in a culture that makes women and girls feel like they're not beautiful. The beauty industry sells us products that are supposed to be the "solution" to our fear, anxiety, shame, and feelings of ugliness.

As much as I love lipstick, I'm sorry to report that beauty products are never, ever going to get rid of these feelings. Only we can.

There's a saying in marketing: "Sell to the pain." That pain includes things like fear of loneliness, fear of not feeling attractive, fear of never finding a partner, fear of being judged in public, fear of looking like you don't have money, fear of having curly hair, fear of having skin that's "too dark," fear of having skin that's "too fair," fear of someone knowing you're on your period, fear of someone knowing that you fart, fear of body hair, fear of aging, and the list goes on and on. We're taught to be afraid of all the stuff that makes us human, unique, and interesting.

6. Thin does *not* equal beautiful

I used to exercise several hours a day and be terrified of food, because I was taught that being fat is the worst thing a person can be. Especially if you're a girl.

In our culture, we're taught that we should marry a man and that he should be bigger than us. Not true. We are taught that thinness is the same as beauty and that fatness is the same as ugliness. Also not true.

We're going to talk about fatphobia in Chapter 3, but for now let me just say that every body exists the exact way it's meant to exist. You don't need to worry about what your body looks like. You need to worry about living your best life on *your* terms.

7. It is not your job to be beautiful

We are taught to believe that a "real" woman is a beautiful woman. From day one we comment on how baby girls look, and it never ends from there on out. The truth is that it's not your job to be pretty or anyone else's idea of beautiful. It's your job to be *you*, to pursue the things you're passionate about, to defend your body against verbal and physical harm, to learn about the things that matter to you, to take care of your friends, to advocate for yourself, and to stay away from people who don't see or care about you.

8. Wanting love is not a reason to pursue beauty ideals

Women and girls are taught that we have to *earn* love by being pretty. I'm here to tell you: that's ridiculous and it's not true.

I know that in movies and stuff, the people (usually dudes) who go after beautiful girls and women seem totally awesome! They have great hair. They are charming. They have amazing shoes. Their teeth are so bright. They're funny.

In real life, though, a person who goes after someone because of how they look is typically an insecure and selfish person who needs a lot of validation from other people because they have no love for themselves. Their love is conditional.

Hard truth: love that is conditional on how you look isn't love at all. It's a form of manipulation, control, and abuse. These things hurt us.

Actual love is about seeing the goodness in another person, being honest with them, setting boundaries if they aren't acting right, wanting them to thrive, and not attempting to make their existence about your needs.

I know that everything you've ever read or seen tells you that if you become what society deems beautiful you will find love, but I'm here to

> Hard truth: love that is conditional on how you look isn't love at all.

tell you it's not true. When I was obsessed with following all the beauty rules, I kept thinking about all the amazing people I was going to be able to date when I finally got my "dream body." That whole time, I was missing a huge, important secret: anyone who needs you to look a certain way in order to pay attention to you is actually a total jerk—they're actually not amazing at all. You don't want them in your life, Girl. Period.

I've met the best partners after I stopped following all the beauty rules. I fell in love with them because they wanted me to live my best life for me, not look like a model for them.

9. Beauty standards weren't designed to benefit girls or women—they were designed to control us

As you read at the very beginning of this chapter, beauty standards have led to foot-binding and women's inability to walk in China, neck-lengthening that creates lifelong discomfort in Thailand and Burma, force-feeding in Mauritania and Niger, and an obsession with eating as little as possible in the United States. Do any of these things benefit the women who are going through so much to achieve their culture's idea of beauty? What do you think?

write About It

Take a few seconds to think about what you consider beautiful. Where did you learn it? Who taught you? How long did it take for you to learn it?

2

Question the Culture

A culture is made up of people, places, language, history, media, and customs. It's also made up of ideas—some of which are amazing and some of which really aren't.

We live in a culture that promotes and upholds a lot of problematic ideas: sexism (the idea that men are better than women), racism (the idea that white people are better than all other races), ableism (the idea that an able-bodied person is better than a disabled person), classism (the idea that rich people are better than poor people), homophobia (the idea that straight people are better than queer people), and body shame and fatphobia (the idea that thin people are better than fat people), to name a few. All of these things have to do with our bodies in some way.

Questioning the culture means questioning things like why girls wear waist trainers, why it's okay to make jokes about fat people, or why we think expensive stuff makes people important.

I'm sure you've noticed that there are a lot of messages we get all the time—at school, at home, in movies, in music videos, and online—that tell us there is something wrong with the way we look. Maybe we feel too big, too small, too bony, too tall, not feminine enough, too hairy, too dark, or too light. Even the people we think of as "perfect" often have a lot of pain and shame around their body. Why? Because we live in a culture that teaches us to feel like this. Women in particular get nonstop feedback on how they look. We live in a culture where it's completely okay for mass media and individuals to tell us about ourselves.

People tell us what they think of how our body looks in certain clothes.

People tell us what looks good or bad on our bodies.

People tell us what we should and shouldn't eat.

People tell us we'd look better with makeup.

People tell us how they think our hair looks.

People make fun of us for no good reason.

People give us unsolicited advice on how to lose—or gain—weight.

People tell us that if we don't do certain things, no one will love us.

Why aren't people telling us how amazing we look, that love should not be conditional on looks, that we are more than just our bodies, and that we should eat what we want and wear what we want? Because we don't live in a culture that condones those kinds of ideas. We live in a culture that promotes body shame and judgment.

You might feel a little hopeless after reading all that (or maybe you feel affirmed because you sensed that this stuff was happening). I want you to know that there's nothing hopeless about any of this. It's a beautiful thing when you look at the truth around you and admit it's happening.

Never be afraid of the truth. Be afraid of lying to yourself and to others.

You have the power to change all of this—maybe not for everyone in the whole wide world, but for you and the people around you. Start with you and your friends.

Start by asking these five questions about any popular or widely believed idea:

1. How does this cultural idea make me feel?

2. Who benefits from this cultural idea?

3. What is this cultural idea trying to do?

4. Does this cultural idea benefit me and the people I care about?

5. Do I want to keep investing in this behavior or product?

Let's ask these questions about something I mentioned earlier—waist trainers, which are garments designed to force your body into the shape of an hourglass. I'll offer example answers.

Cultural idea: girls and women look better when they're wearing waist trainers.

1. How does this cultural idea make me feel?

It makes me feel like it's my job to make my body look a certain way in order to be considered beautiful or sexy.

2. Who benefits from this cultural idea?

At first I thought I did, because people always give me compliments when I wear a waist trainer, and that makes me feel good in the moment. Actually, though, I realized that this idea really benefits the companies that make shaping garments, and maybe it also benefits others who feel uncomfortable seeing that we all have different body shapes.

3. What is this cultural idea trying to do?

It's trying to keep me in my place and keep me small. It's trying to make it seem normal that I should have to spend extra money on waist trainers and be uncomfortable all day wearing them. This is sexist.

4. Does this cultural idea benefit me and the people I care about?

Nope.

5. Do I want to keep investing in this behavior or product?

Kind of yes and kind of no. It makes me feel more sexy and less self-conscious. I like the compliments people give me when I'm wearing one. But I also recognize that I don't need to wear one, and it feels uncomfortable sometimes when I sit down or when I eat. I'm going to read more about the history of shapewear and think about how much more comfortable my daily life could be without a waist trainer.

Bring these five questions with you as you interact in the world. It's easier to start with the media you're already looking at. If you're following someone or something on social media that makes you feel bad, you can unfollow and unsubscribe from it. Find things that make you feel good and okay. If you're buying things that you feel don't actually benefit you or people you care about, then consider buying less or none of them. Invest in the things that you genuinely want and need.

Another powerful way that harmful ideas get spread and promoted is through advertising—things like commercials and pop-up ads.

I mentioned before this saying in advertising: "Sell to the pain."

What does that mean exactly?

In the world of business, "pain" can mean different things. It can be used instead of the word "problem." A problem that needs solving is a pain. So a "pain" might be that someone has ants all over their kitchen and they really hate ants. If you have a product that gets rid of ants, you can sell that product by talking about the pain of having ants in your house.

"Pain" can go deeper than that, though. For a lot of young women, advertisers are selling to the "pain" of dissatisfaction with how they look, how they feel about their body, or their fear of being rejected. So selling to that pain means reminding someone of those insecurities in order to get them to buy something that might soothe that fear—temporarily. You can probably think of about one trillion examples of this, but I'll offer some:

We are taught the myth that body hair is unfeminine, so some ads for hair removal products remind you of the "pain" of someone seeing your leg or underarm hair.

We are taught the myth that higher body weight is unattractive, so ads for weight-control products remind you of the "pain" of feeling unlovable.

We are taught the myth that straight hair looks better than curly hair, so ads for hair products remind you of the "pain" of feeling like something is wrong with your natural hair texture.

We are taught the myth that skin with no pimples, blemishes, or marks is normal, so ads for skin care products remind you of the "pain" of feeling like something is wrong with you.

We are taught the myth that rich people are better than poor people, so ads for clothing or shoes remind you of the "pain" of feeling like you don't have enough.

A lot of unexpected things rely on money from marketing and advertising. Did you know that movies rely on money from advertising? And so do magazines, social media, and search engines. A lot of things that are free still need money to pay for the employees and equipment they need to function. This is a big deal because, since they're paying the bills, advertisers get to make important decisions about what is in the magazine or the movie or the social media. If you've ever heard the line "The advertisers aren't gonna like this!" in a movie, this is what they're talking about.

Let's look at an example of this. Let's say I own a company that sells diet pills. I want to put an ad in a magazine for my pills. Who wants to lose weight?

Well, because of fatphobia, pretty much everyone in the United States does. But if I look at some statistics I can quickly tell that women spend a lot more money on weight-loss products than other people do. So I decide I'm going to put the ad in a magazine that women read.

I approach the magazine and ask them how much it costs to put an ad right in the front of the next issue, maybe on page 1, 2, or 3. They tell me it costs $10,000.

That's a lot of money, right? If I'm paying all that money I intend to make all that money back, as well as a profit. I agree to the amount of money, but if I'm going to invest that much, I want to make sure that there aren't articles in the magazine that are critical of weight-loss products, because that's going to make it less likely that I will sell my pills. So I tell the person in charge at the magazine that if I'm going to invest, then I want to be able to have a say about what else appears in the magazine. The magazine needs that $10,000, so they agree. If you've ever needed money really bad, you can probably relate to this feeling.

This is what marketing and advertising were designed to do—encourage people to buy things. The problem is that marketers learned that you could get people to buy a lot more if you reminded them of their pain—fear that they aren't pretty, insecurity that they might not find a partner, loneliness, or the sense that their body isn't right.

Sometimes the ad doesn't use negative language and instead uses "inspiration" to get you to buy. But images of slender, light-skinned, or athletic women can activate the fear that we aren't good enough. Images of women in blissfully happy relationships, traveling to international destinations, wearing designer clothes, and eating expensive food can activate fear that we aren't trying hard enough.

Advertising isn't pure evil, but it's important to question it, because it doesn't always have your best interests at heart. Speaking of ads, I want to tell you a story about a small change I made to media I was consuming and how it impacted me in a big way.

I like getting my nails done. Nail art is my thing. I'll get a Halloween-themed manicure that's orange and black or a Christmas pedicure with red sparkles. My nails make me feel visible as a big brown woman and allow me to express myself. Other people who like nails talk to me, and I get to meet strangers who want to geek out over colors and styles. Ever since I was a little girl, I used to admire the women I saw at the salon, and when I finally got a job after high school, cool nails were one of the first things I invested in.

One of the things I *always* saw other women doing at the salon was reading *Us Weekly* and *People*. At pretty much any nail salon in the United States, you can walk in and find a stack of magazines that are about women. Most of the articles are about actresses' divorces, cheating, weight loss, weight gain, plastic surgery, babies, clothes, purses, makeup, and shoes. Sometimes there's a piece about books or other accomplishments, but the magazines focus a lot on criticizing women's bodies and decisions.

Reading those magazines felt like a rite of passage when I started going to the salon. Reading them made me feel like I was part of a secret society of Babes Who Loved Nails. So every time I went in, I read one or two from cover to cover. I didn't really think about how they made me feel. I just kind of zombied out, mimicking the women around me.

And then one day something changed. I noticed that with each page and article and ad, I felt worse and worse about myself. I felt like my body was wrong. I felt like I was too big. I felt like I didn't have enough money. I felt like I hadn't accomplished anything. I felt like I had failed because I wasn't married to a supermodel dude. I definitely felt like I needed $300 for Tom Ford perfume that I couldn't afford.

I realized that I had direct control over changing this tiny habit that impacted me in a big way. So I made a promise to myself: no more magazines like those. Not in my house. Not in my car. And not even when I was getting my nails done. I could read something else, or I could just relax. That was the rule. I haven't read a single entertainment magazine since. I get cultural messaging all the time about myself—that's unavoidable—but reading magazines was totally in the realm of my control.

Tip: always figure out whether someone or something has your best interests at heart.

Answering the questions below will help you determine whether someone or something is looking out for you. In general, huge companies are not. You get to make your own decisions about how you want to interact with them if you figure out that they don't care about you. When you're watching something, reading something, or scrolling through something, ask yourself:

How does this make me feel?

Who benefits from this content?

What are they selling me?

What "pain" are they trying to activate, to get me to spend money?

Does this benefit me and the people I care about?

write About It

What's one small thing you can get rid of right now that can positively change how you feel about your body? It might be unfollowing things or people that make you feel bad about yourself. It might mean no longer saying negative things about your body to your friends.

3

Fatphobia and How It Hurts Your Body Image

I used to hate being fat.

Like really, really hated it. I fantasized about getting out of bed in the middle of the night while my family was asleep, walking to the kitchen, pulling a huge butcher knife out of the drawer, and cutting all my fat off. That's how much I hated being fat.

But the weird thing was, I hadn't always felt that way. When I was a little kid I used to love being fat. I used to jiggle my body, and take all my clothes off as often as I could, and run around naked. I didn't have any negative feelings about my body whatsoever.

One day when I was four years old, a boy in my class called me "fat." I had never heard that word before then, but I knew it was a bad word because of the way he said it. He said it like I had done something wrong. Not long after that boy said it, all the boys started to say it. By the time I was done with kindergarten I had learned that I was fat, and that being fat was the worst thing I could ever be.

For a very long time I blamed myself for being fat.

I thought I didn't have enough self-control to just eat less or run more. Other people hated me because of my body, and that made me hate myself and my body. When I was a little older, I met a bunch of activists who taught me that I wasn't bad. They taught me that what I experienced was abusive and oppressive. They said the people who hated me were wrong. And they taught me that what I had experienced had a name: fatphobia.

Fatphobia is a form of discrimination, similar to sexism and racism.

We learn fatphobia from our peers, our families, ads, shows, and movies. Fatphobia teaches us that fat people are bad, stupid, ugly, and unhealthy. It says that fat people aren't as good as thin people. Fatphobia makes people afraid of gaining weight or being big. Fatphobia makes people spend billions of dollars on gyms and diet products. And it makes it seem like it's totally normal to be mean to fat people, when actually it's not totally normal to be mean to someone because of their body.

Fatphobia—like all forms of discrimination or oppression—is based on the make-believe idea that some people are better than others. The idea behind fatphobia is that fat is really bad and that thin is really good. Fatphobia divides people into groups—the "good" guys and the "bad" guys—and then pits them against each other.

Fatphobia especially affects women, because we live in a culture where women are expected to be small, quiet, weak, and frail—and are rewarded for being those things.

Fatphobia negatively affects how we think of our bodies in a ton of ways:

1. It makes us feel worthless.

2. It makes us feel like we are never small enough.

3. It makes us afraid of our body.

4. It makes us afraid of food.

5. It makes us feel like we can't trust our body.

6. It makes us question our hunger signals.

7. It makes us obsess about what we eat.

8. It makes us feel like no matter what we do in order to lose weight, it's worth it—even if it's unpleasant or self-harming.

9. It makes us feel like something is wrong with our bodies.

10. It makes us feel like we have to compete with other girls.

11. It makes us compare ourselves to other people.

12. It makes us think that if we aren't thin, we don't deserve love and respect from others.

13. It makes us think that we have to lose weight if we want to date or get married.

Fatphobia ruled my life for a really long time because I believed that my body was wrong and bad, and I was willing to do almost anything to change it. It took me a while, but I finally found people who looked like me and were living totally amazing lives. They taught me that nothing was wrong with my body. And they taught me that being fat wasn't bad—it was rad.

"Fat" is a word that makes a lot of people feel kind of awkward. If you're like most people, you've been taught that the word "fat" is mean and impolite.

It's true that many people don't like being described as fat, but I do. I use the word to describe myself because I used to be really terrified of that word. "Fat" was a word that was used to silence me and make me feel ashamed of myself. The word had a lot of power, and I lived in fear that someone would say it to me, or even *around* me.

When I was afraid of being fat, I was obsessed with how much I ate and exercised. I would sometimes starve myself for weeks, only eating a few bites of food each day. I made myself pretty sick, but I was sure that it was worth it because everyone told me that I should do anything to become thin. Everyone told me that deep down I was a thin person, and I just needed to work hard to free my "real" self.

It turns out that they were super wrong. I am not bad at being thin. My body was meant to be fat.

I was tired of being afraid of a word. So I decided to reclaim "fat" and make it my own. A lot of other groups of people who have been made to feel shame have reclaimed the words they were afraid of, like "queer" or "black" or "cripple."

Fatphobia is really good at making us afraid. You've probably already heard all the arguments that being fat is unhealthy and makes you sick. What we never hear about is how research clearly shows that it's almost impossible for a naturally fat person to lose enough weight to be considered thin. The Huffington Post shared in an article that the chances of a fat woman becoming a thin woman is 0.8 percent. Just to be totally clear, that's less than 1 percent. We never hear the research that states that people don't actually "lose" weight; they almost always gain it back. We never hear about the research that states that dieting makes people depressed and anxious. And we never hear about the research that states that fat people have advantages over thin people—like we have stronger muscles—and one study showed that fatter patients lived longer after chemotherapy treatment for a certain kind of cancer than thinner patients did.[2] There have always been bigger people and smaller people in every human society. There has not always been discrimination against bigger people, though.

If we decide to get rid of the discrimination—fatphobia—there's no more fear. It's actually pretty simple. You can decide right now that you're not going to make fun of fat people or treat fat people poorly. You can decide you're not going to treat someone who's fat any different than someone who's thin. You can decide right now that you're going to speak up when fatphobia happens. If we all did that, we could end fatphobia overnight. It's way, way easier to stop being fatphobic than it is for a fat person to become a thin person.

Here are some common questions about fat, fat-shaming, and fatphobia and how they affect body image.

Is it okay to call someone "fat"?

It's important to ask someone what words you can use to describe them. Some people like the word "fat" and some people don't.

What are examples of fatphobia?

I think of fatphobia as something that happens on three different levels:

1. **Interpersonal**—when a person or group of people hates on a person who's fat. Examples of interpersonal fatphobia are when someone calls a fat person a degrading name or when someone refuses to date someone because they're fat.

2. **Intrapersonal**—when a person has negative ideas or feelings about themselves. Examples of intrapersonal fatphobia are when someone is constantly criticizing the fat parts of their body or engaging in eating or exercise habits designed to make someone as thin as possible.

3. **Institutional or cultural**—when the culture makes it hard for a fat person to function in society. Examples of institutional or cultural fatphobia are when a classroom only has small desks or when a clothing store only carries small sizes.

Is everyone affected by fatphobia?

Yes, but we're all affected differently. So, a thin person might have a lot of body shame, but they do not experience the cultural part of fatphobia, like not being able to fit in a small airplane seat. A fat person might have a lot of body shame, and they also experience the cultural side.

There are different kinds of fat people. Some people are considered fat by their family but aren't considered fat by people outside their home, or vice versa. Some people are fat but they can still shop in most stores and fit in most airplane or classroom seats. And some people are fat and don't have access to comfortable seating or clothes.

I have engaged in fatphobic behavior. What do I do?

If you have been engaging in fatphobic behavior or thoughts, you can make the choice to change. You can apologize to people you have hurt and do your best moving forward.

Does fatphobia exist all over the world?

No. Fatphobia is really common in North America, Europe, and Australia as well as many countries in South America, Central America, and Asia. Different regions in the US have different views on fat. If you live in a big and wealthy city, like New York or San Francisco, the body ideal is often much slimmer and more athletic than in the Midwest and the South.

There are several regions of the world where fat is considered normal or even particularly attractive. The first time I ever visited a place where fat was normal, it totally blew my mind. I went to this small island in the Pacific Ocean near New Zealand called Rarotonga; it's part of a chain of islands called the Cook Islands. Most of the people in the Cook Islands are Polynesian, and their bodies are big and glorious.

And as mentioned earlier, in parts of Mauritania and Niger, women are encouraged to be as fat as possible. Sometimes young women are forced to eat a lot of really rich food by older women, because the fatter a woman is, the likelier she is to get married. The people in these cultures view fatness as a sign of beauty and wealth.

Whether a culture promotes fatness or thinness, it is usually women who suffer in order to meet an unrealistic and unfair beauty ideal. In the parts of the world where women are expected to be fat, some of them die or get sick by doing whatever they have to do to be as fat as possible. Similarly, in parts of the world where women are expected to be thin, some die or get sick from doing whatever they have to do to be as thin as possible.

What is dieting?

Dieting means eating less food or special kinds of food in order to lose weight.

What's an eating disorder?

This is sort of hard to answer because I see disordered eating as eating in a way that causes anxiety or stress. But it can be defined as a set of behaviors and beliefs that make a person engage in abnormal or obsessive eating habits that negatively affect their physical or mental health. A lot of people are very worried about what they eat and how much they eat. So even though an estimated one in five women have an eating disorder,[3] I think there's a good chance the number is much higher.

Can people of color have eating disorders?

Yes, absolutely. Most movies, shows, and books about eating disorders focus on thin, young white women. This leads to the belief that only thin, young white women have eating disorders, but that isn't true. This myth harms people of color, because they might have an eating disorder and not even know it.

Can fat people have eating disorders?

Yes, definitely. Unfortunately, because the only representations of eating disorders we have are of very thin (usually white) women, many fat people have eating disorders and don't know it. For example, I went through periods of engaging in anorexic behavior, but because I am fat and brown, I didn't think there was any way that I was anorexic.

If we don't use weight as a way to tell if someone is healthy, then what can we use?

Well, to begin with, every single person deserves to live a life without discrimination, no matter their weight or health status. We should not base our behavior or attitudes on whether we think someone is "healthy" or not. There are many people of all sizes with chronic illnesses. It's not our job to decide whether someone is healthy. It's our job to be kind and compassionate to all people.

There's an idea called "weight neutrality" or "health at every size" (HAES, for short), which is asking people to stop looking at weight as an indicator of health and to stop pressuring people to lose weight.

In general, the science is pretty clear—trying to control your weight doesn't work.[4] When a study says that weight loss leads to better health, it is often leaving out important information. For instance, in a study about weight and heart health, they'll have people do exercise and eat more vegetables—and guess what? Their heart health improves. In some people that might lead to temporary weight loss, but rather than saying "eating vegetables and exercising is good for your heart," they'll say "weight loss is good for your heart." This is sloppy research! We also know that when people experience discrimination and cruelty it makes their blood pressure go up,[5] it makes them sad, and that makes them more susceptible to illness. These are bad things that we can prevent if we stop engaging in fatphobia.

When people have access to nutritious food, and places where they can move their bodies, and they don't experience discrimination, they live better lives no matter how much they weigh.

Are fat people healthy?

There are fat people who have overall good health and fat people who don't—just like there are thin people who have overall good health and thin people who don't. What makes someone "healthy" is complicated and takes into account things like genetics, how much money they have, what kind of grocery stores they have access to, how safe their neighborhood is, and whether they're experiencing abuse—at home, at school, or at work. Fat people often have stronger muscles because we are lifting and holding up our bodies all the time. I have a friend who got into a terrible car accident, and the only reason she didn't die was because the fat in her stomach prevented her steering wheel from hitting her internal organs.

There are lots of things that fat bodies do that are unique and important. At the end of the day, we have to remember that whether someone is "healthy" or not, we shouldn't have negative thoughts about or behaviors toward them.

How can I stop being fatphobic?

You can stop using the word "fat" as a negative word. You can read books about fat activism and HAES. You can stop criticizing your own body and the bodies of others. Remember: fatphobia makes your body into the enemy, when your body is actually your most important ally.

Write About It

Which level(s) of fatphobia affects you—interpersonal, intrapersonal, or institutional/cultural? Choose one fatphobic behavior you engage in. Take some time to write about where you learned it from, how it harms you, and how it affects others. How can you stop doing that behavior?

4

Racism Affects How You Think of Your Body

A few years ago I went to Bangkok, the largest city in Thailand. Bangkok is an amazing place, full of bright pink taxis, perfectly ripe dragon fruit, and monks in marigold robes. I saw a lot of things in Bangkok that I'd never seen anywhere else—like baby tigers and people cooking roaches on skewers to sell for a few Baht (the currency in Thailand) as a snack.

I also saw skin-lightening products for the first time in my life.

They were everywhere. There were skin-lightening chemicals or oils in most face washes, body washes, and lotions available in any store that sold bath products. I even found a nipple-lightening cream! It was hard to find a body product that *didn't* market its lightening qualities. I read the labels, which were often in English and Thai. Some of them guaranteed that the product painlessly removed "old" skin and left "newer," "younger"-looking skin. It was interesting that they used words like "old" to talk about brown skin and "young" or "new" to talk about light skin.

In a 2018 article in the British newspaper *The Guardian*, Coco Khan wrote: "In 2017, the global skin-lightening industry was worth

$4.8 billion....Skin-lightening products include creams, scrubs, pills, and even injections designed to slow the production of melanin. Many of these are created by pharmaceutical giants such as Unilever, Proctor and Gamble, and L'Oréal and come with massive marketing budgets. A World Health Organization study found that 40 percent of Chinese women regularly use skin-lightening creams. That number is 61 percent in India and 77 percent in Nigeria."[6]

I used to be embarrassed about the parts of my body that were darker.

I thought something was wrong with me because I never saw anyone whose body looked like mine on TV or in any of the movies I watched. All the people I admired in shows and movies were white people. Every man who was portrayed as a hero or a hottie was white. Every woman who was portrayed as smart or sexy was white. I was surrounded by images of thin white people, or people of color who were very light and very thin.

So even though I didn't want skin-lightening products, I understood why they existed. I had been taught that light skin was more desirable.

Though I never tried to lighten my skin, I did experiment with lightening my hair and my eye color. When I was eighteen I decided I wanted to dye my hair for the first time, and almost bought green eye contacts. In my head I told myself I just wanted something "different," but the truth is, I wanted lighter hair and eyes because I thought my dark features weren't unique or special. I saw lighter hair and eyes as more beautiful and interesting.

Despite all this, for a long time I believed that racism didn't affect me.

I thought racism was only when someone called a person of color a horrible name or was part of the KKK. Robin DiAngelo explains in her book *White Fragility: Why It's So Hard for White People to Talk About Racism* that in the United States, many people believe that racism is always obvious and intentional. But the truth is, it's often neither.

Yes, people wearing white hoods and calling someone an "illegal" are definitely examples of racism, but this is not the only way racism presents itself. Actually, most of the time it doesn't look like this at all.

There are lots of other ways that racism manifests. Racism might affect how we feel about our hair, our skin tone, and the shape of our body (because we've been taught that white bodies are the ideal). We see it in the way the world works—like how most movies and best-selling books are about white people, most people in prison are people of color, and most CEOs are white men.

But racism isn't just attitudes that other people have. It also exists inside us, in our subconscious.

It manifests in attitudes—like the way that teachers are stricter with brown and black kids or the way that brown and black people are often called "loud" when they're just having fun. It manifests in preferences—like how people in the US love French and British accents but hate accents from places where the people are brown or black.

For people of color, there's a third dimension to racism: it manifests in how we see ourselves, our potential, our beauty, and our worth.

Yes, these are all facts you might already know about, but the thing I didn't know for a long time was that those things really affected me in a big way. They affected how I felt, how I saw my body, how I saw my future, and how I saw people who looked like me. Racism taught me who was better and who was inferior, who was pretty and who was ugly, who mattered and who didn't, and who I was taught to be attracted to and what I felt like I deserved as a brown girl.

I didn't know how to see racism—or how it impacted me—because it didn't look the way I thought it did. I thought it would be super obvious if I felt racist feelings toward myself or others. But that's not how it works *most* of the time.

I realized racism is less like a cold, and more like a cancer. If you have a cold, you know you have a cold. You sneeze, your nose is stuffed, you can't taste things, and your head hurts. You know without a doubt when you get hit with a cold. Cancer is different. Some people go years without knowing they have it. It often doesn't hurt for a really long time. There aren't obvious symptoms all the time. And it takes special tools to be able to detect it sometimes.

In 1970, a black professor at Harvard named Chester M. Pierce came up with a word for some of these more subtle racist moments. The word is "microaggressions."

According to Derald Wing Sue, PhD, microaggressions are "everyday verbal, nonverbal, and environmental slights, snubs, or insults, whether intentional or unintentional, which communicate hostile, derogatory, or negative messages to target persons based solely upon their marginalized group membership."[7] The prefix "micro" means "extremely small." An extremely small aggression might look like:

- People never pronouncing your name correctly

- People constantly asking where you're from ("No, where are you *really* from?")

- People randomly switching into a foreign language (like when people use "hola" in conversations with me—because I'm Latinx—but not with anyone else)

- People pointing out or being surprised by how "eloquent" you are

These small aggressions add up over time, impacting your life, how you view yourself, and how you view the world.

Racism affects how we think of our bodies in sometimes weird and unexpected ways.

Sometimes we don't even realize we're experiencing or engaging in racism because we don't use the word "race" or talk about it explicitly. Kind of like how the skin-lightening cream in Bangkok used the word "old" instead of the word "dark."

Here's another example. Eyelid surgery is the most common cosmetic surgery request in Asia.[8] A plastic surgeon makes one cut on each upper eyelid in a short procedure, and the patient leaves with a fold or crease in the eye that makes the eye appear larger. About half of all East Asians are born with a monolid—an eyelid without a fold.[9] An eyelid with a crease is more common among people of European descent.

One plastic surgeon in China said in an interview that most of her patients were women aged seventeen to twenty-eight.[10] The women who get the surgery often report that they think the eyelid surgery makes them more "attractive" or allows them to use new makeup techniques that were designed for eyelids with a crease; they almost all use words like "attractive" or "better" to talk about getting this surgery that makes their eyes look more European. None of the women talk about race. Do you see how this is similar to using words like "young" and "old" instead of "light" and "dark"?

In South Korea, another plastic surgery is popular—calf reduction. Some of the ads for the surgery say that Korean women have thicker calves than Caucasian women, but many just use words like "sexier" or "slimmer" to describe the benefits of calf reduction. "Slim," "young," and "sexy" aren't racial words, and yet achieving European features are often the goal.

It's important to listen to your instincts when you think racism is happening

The first time I felt racism in a really big way was when I moved away from home and moved into the dorms at my college. It was the first time in my life that I was surrounded by primarily white people. Even though no one said anything obviously racist to me, I felt in my gut that I didn't belong. I didn't understand this gut feeling because I'd lived my whole life around other brown and black people. I began to read books about racism, and that's when I learned that other people of color felt this same sense of loneliness and rejection in primarily white spaces. What I was feeling had real effects on my mental health, even though no one ever called me a name or said I didn't belong.

In 2018, I spoke to some young women of color at a San Francisco high school, and they told me they'd noticed an important way that racism manifested at their school. They said they noticed that white girls were treated as if they needed to be kept safe and protected, and the girls I was talking to felt they were not given that same consideration or care. Young women and girls of color often experience something called "adultification,"[11] when adults or peers view someone as less innocent and more adult-like. Adultification includes the belief that girls of color need less emotional support and know more about mature topics like sexuality.

Like beauty (which I talked about in Chapter 1), racism is not something we are born understanding—we learn it through our culture. It's important to recognize that racism is not our fault, and that we can still feel powerful about our bodies and our lives. We can celebrate our skin, hair, shape, shade, and unique perspective on the world.

As a girl or young woman of color, you have extraordinary gifts.

Navigating racism is painful and frustrating, but it gives us a unique perspective on the culture and ourselves. Every culture has its problems, and when we're honest about the fact that racism is one of the biggest problems in the US, we are in a good position to figure out how we want to deal with it.

Some people reclaim the words that have been used to hurt or shame them. Some people start hashtags at their school, like one Filipino tenth-grader I met who used #FilipinoPride to flag his identity at a primarily white high school. Some people reclaim their hair and accentuate its natural curl and wave. And some people don't do any of that and instead choose to hold their understanding within themselves.

As a girl or young woman of color, you have extraordinary gifts.

write About It

What are ways that you and your friends show up proudly as people of color? Have you experienced microaggressions or seen them happen around you? Write about one or two instances and the impact they had on you.

5

We've Been Obsessing About Food for More Than 200 Years

Many people are afraid of what they eat, how much they eat, and when they eat.

They're afraid of what food will do to their bodies. They're afraid that they eat too much. They're afraid that food will make them sick. They're afraid of food with fat in it. They're afraid of butter, dessert, and anything with whipped cream on it. They're afraid of sugar. They're afraid of soda. They're afraid of bacon. They're afraid when they eat and don't exercise right after. They're afraid of what might happen if they don't control everything they eat. They're afraid of their desire for food. They think certain foods are "good" and other foods are "evil."

Every day we learn from the culture around us that it's normal to have an obsessive relationship with food. Why? Because in our culture we equate eating food with being fat, and because of fatphobia, we equate being fat with being bad.

I used to be terrified of food. I hated feeling hungry. I hated feeling full. I hated how eating made me feel. I had been taught that food was bad because food made people fat.

I thought I was just a weirdo, but then I started to notice that I wasn't the only one. And I started to notice something kinda creepy: everyone around me was totally obsessed with food too. No matter what size they were, they were always talking about it, thinking about it, and acting strange around cookies and cake. And most of the time, it wasn't fun or positive. They weren't talking about how great burgers are, or those delicious mashed potatoes their mom made, or how much they loved milkshakes. They were talking about food like it was a monster in a scary movie.

Our culture promotes an obsessive and fear-based relationship to food, and it's not okay.

Let me just set the record straight for one second: hunger is a normal human instinct. Food is not evil or scary. We need food. We need a lot of food! Humans are pretty big animals, with complex brains and muscles. We need energy to keep those things running and working well. You don't need to be afraid of food or hunger, or what your body will do when you put food into it.

Yes, the rumors about vegetables being good for you are true, but your brain also needs sugar and starch and fat to function. Literally. Your body *needs* stuff with fat in it. Your brain is 60 percent fat.[12] Fatty acids—the building blocks of the fat in food and our bodies—are crucial for your brain's ability to perform.[13] Your body converts sugar and starch into energy that you need to stay awake and alert.

Your body thrives when you aren't hungry and it has enough food.

And different bodies respond to food differently. Some people eat a bunch and stay super thin, and some people don't eat a bunch and are fat. That's because body size is mostly about genetics, not how you eat.[14] Body diversity is a good thing! Body shape is almost entirely biologically determined, and all bodies are good bodies.

So where do all of our weirdo ideas about food come from? Answer: a lot of places, but I want to tell you about two old white dudes who played a big role in how we think of food today. Ready?

Once upon a time there was an old white dude named Sylvester. He was born in 1794 in Connecticut, which is on the East Coast of the US. He really, super hated sex. He was sure that sex was going to lead to the fall of our country, and he had a few ideas about how to deal with the growing number

> Your body thrives when you aren't hungry and it has enough food.

of pervs he thought were living in the US: he believed that yummy food led to sexual behavior, and that if we could control what we ate, we could control our sexuality.

In the mid-1800s Sylvester started this thing called the Dietary Reform Movement.[15] He and his followers promoted food that had very little flavor, very little fat, and no yeast. He was mildly obsessed with crackers because they didn't have yeast in them. I forgot to mention that Sylvester's last name was Graham. Sylvester Graham and his followers invented something called the graham cracker and suggested that people live on a diet of "low-sin" foods. Spices and yummy flavors were off limits. He and his followers were one of the first groups of people who argued that you could control morality through food. They connected how much and what you ate with how good a person you were.

Remember how I told you that fatphobia makes us believe that it's okay to be mean to fat people because fat people are bad? The belief that fat people are "bad" is one of the results of Sylvester's beliefs. As a culture, we believe that fat people eat too much, and we see this as sinful or immoral. It seems natural to us that we'd think this way, but it's actually totally bizarre. There's no logical reason that someone who eats more is a bad person. It could just mean they like food, but because of people like Sylvester Graham, we now accept that they are instead bad—even though that's an idea that he made up.

Another one of my favorite old white dudes to talk about is John Harvey Kellogg. If his name sounds familiar, it's probably because we're still eating something he and his brother invented in 1894—corn flakes.

Like Reverend Graham, Kellogg hated sex, saw it as a threat to our culture, and believed that food was part of the solution to killing people's sex drive. He invented corn flakes as part of a diet that was meant to keep your body—and your soul—clean.[16] He was one of the first major "clean eating" advocates.

Why in the world were two powerful men so obsessed with controlling how much food and sex everyone was enjoying? Well, they were definitely both religious men who were concerned about sin, but let's go deeper. They both lived during a time when the US and some European countries were colonizing other people. During this era of colonialism, mostly white men were going into other countries, enslaving people (slavery was abolished in 1865), stealing land, and forcing people to adopt Christianity. Native Americans were still being slaughtered during this period.

Historian Donald Fixico writes:

> *From the time Europeans arrived on American shores, the*
> *frontier—the edge territory between white man's civilization and*
> *the untamed natural world—became a shared space of vast,*
> *clashing differences that led the U.S. government to authorize*
> *over 1,500 wars, attacks, and raids on Indians, the most of any*
> *country in the world against its indigenous people. By the close of*
> *the Indian Wars in the late 19th century, fewer than 238,000*
> *indigenous people remained, a sharp decline from the estimated*
> *5 million to 15 million living in North America when Columbus*
> *arrived in 1492. The reasons for this racial genocide were*
> *multi-layered. Settlers, most of whom had been barred from*
> *inheriting property in Europe, arrived on American shores*
> *hungry for Indian land—and the abundant natural resources*
> *that came with it... Even more fundamentally, indigenous people*
> *were just too different: Their skin was dark. Their languages*
> *were foreign. And their world views and spiritual beliefs were*
> *beyond most white men's comprehension.*[17]

I want to focus on the last line about worldviews and spiritual beliefs.

Many of the cultures that Americans overtook during colonialism and slavery were cultures that had a more peaceful relationship to food, nature, and sexuality. Many did not believe that sex or food were sinful in the way that Christians did. Many did not believe that they needed to control people. These ideas were considered "savage" and wrong to powerful, Christian white men—like Graham and Kellogg. They *created* the idea that you could be less "savage" by controlling behaviors, like when and how you had sex and when and how you ate.

They invented graham crackers and corn flakes as a way of separating themselves from the black and brown people they were exploiting. They made rules about how they were "good guys" and said that the people who didn't control their body—including what they ate—were "bad guys." Remember how I told you that all oppression stems from creating two groups—good and bad—and pitting them against each other? It's pretty bizarre that our relationship with food today is connected to people who lived a long time ago—and that we're still eating the stuff that they invented!

The idea that controlling how much you eat makes you a "good," "better," or "healthier" person stems from Sylvester and John. Who wants to be considered a "bad" person? Literally no one.

The thing is: being afraid of food totally zaps your power.

What's a powerful response to food? Recognizing that we eat for different reasons. We crave different things.

Eat what you like. Eat when you're hungry. Recognize that you're not a better person if you skip a meal. There's no wrong way to eat. When we stop obsessing about what's going into our body, guess what happens? We stop feeling afraid and can thrive.

After I stopped being obsessed with my body size and decided to love my fat body, I stopped being obsessed with food. Don't get me wrong, I love food—all kinds of food—*a lot*.

I don't think there's one single right way to eat.

We each need different things. We all eat for different reasons. Food has always been part of celebration and mourning. All cultures share food as a way of building community and friendship. We eat because we need to eat, but we also eat when we're feeling sad or happy. We eat for fun. We eat for nourishment. We eat because it feels good. We eat when we are sad. These are normal human behaviors. Eating is good. Food is good.

I'm here to tell you once and for all that no one should ever make you feel bad about how you eat.

People who shame how other people eat are afraid, and they're pushing their fear on others. You have the right to say "How I eat is my business."

write About It

Do you have a good memory of a time you shared food with family or friends? What types of food does your family eat during celebrations? What is your favorite meal?

6

Nine Gross Characteristics of Diet Culture

In 2015, Common Sense Media made headlines by reporting that 80 percent of ten-year-old girls have been on a diet.[18]

Everyone was horrified that this was happening. I was horrified too, but I wasn't surprised—at all. I was on a diet when I was ten. I was taught to hate my body when I was five.

Fatphobia is all around us—at school, at work, at home, on shows, in movies, in advertising, and through the limited sizes of clothing and the tiny seats on airplanes. If you teach someone that fat is bad, and you teach them that they can be thin if they diet, then they are definitely going to diet. It's pretty simple, America.

Like I said in Chapter 3, dieting is when you manipulate what you eat or how much you eat in order to lose weight. Dieting is an individual behavior, but the desire to control how you eat is part of a bigger cultural phenomenon called "diet culture."

Remember how I told you that a culture is made up of people, places, language, history, media, and customs? One of the customs in the US is promoting and normalizing using food in order to manipulate weight. We live in a diet culture. As soon as you're able to watch shows or movies, you become aware of diet culture.

If you think of culture as a fish tank, we are the fish and the culture is the water. It's hard to see water when you're a fish because it's all around you.

Diet culture is a little different from water, though, because fish couldn't survive without water, but we could definitely survive without diet culture. If we don't need it, then why is it there?

The answer to that one is complicated but can be traced back to some of the stuff you've already read about in previous chapters. It goes back to putting people into categories (good and bad; good at obeying diet culture and bad at obeying diet culture) and the history of controlling people in order to get them to do things that benefit a small group of people in power—the same way that those companies get you to buy stuff so they can make more money.

I think it helps to talk about what diet culture looks like so you can know how to spot it. Here are nine characteristics of diet culture that I've observed.

1. You learn about diet culture when you're a kid

Researchers have found that children in the US are already aware that weight gain and fatness are negative. And it turns out that when you learn something in childhood, it's hard to unlearn it unless you are taught something different (such as the things in this very book, Girl).

2. You learn to be more concerned about what others think of you than how you feel or what *you* want

Diet culture is about making us believe that there is one—and only one—ideal body type. This is really weird, because people look different depending on where they come from, their ancestors, and their unique genes. Diet culture is about making conformity seem normal. Each of us is an incredible, wonderful, beautiful individual, but we forget that all the time. Our culture tells everybody to be thin—no matter what their parents or ancestors looked like—and that is just super weird. The truth is: conformity does not nourish us or make us happy, in the end. Honoring who we really are—including our body, exactly as it is—does.

3. You learn that calorie-counting and shame about eating is normal

Humans haven't always counted calories and grams of fat. Being obsessed with how fattening everything is can be pretty destructive and can lead to anxiety and depression. Thanksgiving, Christmas, and other holidays are considered "indulgent" or "feasting" days. This tradition goes back to the Romans. Feasting days play an important role in our culture—they are days when the entire culture can "let loose" or let off a little steam so that they can return to being disciplined and well behaved during non-holidays. This models—on a cultural scale—dieting behavior.

4. You learn to compliment people if they look like they've lost weight—and to have minimal concerns about how it happened

If you've ever lost weight, you might have noticed that people give you lots of compliments. I remember being an eleven-year-old who lost a bunch of weight because I had starved myself for three months; when I went to the doctor, he told me I looked great and did not seem worried at all that an eleven-year-old who was going through puberty had rapidly changed weight. Troubling! If he had asked me how or why my weight loss had happened, I would have answered: 1. Deprivation, 2. Self-hatred. This complete lack of concern for how an outcome is achieved is a big problem that makes eating disorders less visible.

5. Diet culture takes the fun out of moving and eating

This is a big one. Exercise is just movement. Diet is just food. Humans have always, always had an intimate relationship to movement and food. Through diet culture these natural features of life are turned into activities that we can use to lose weight. Moving and eating can give people pleasure, bring us together, and nourish and comfort us. When you focus on joy—rather than on changing the way your body looks—you restore that natural relationship to these things. An amazing thing I learned by talking to a nutritionist researcher was that depending on our mood, we absorb the nutrition in food differently. If we are happy, we are more likely to absorb nutrients! So you could set the same meal in front of ten people, and their bodies will do different things with that food depending on how they feel.

6. Diet culture puts food and body size into categories of good and bad

Calling someone's body size or food "good" or "bad" is...weird. I know we've been taught it's normal, but take a step back and think about how unusual this is. The truth is, no one is better or worse for being bigger or smaller. Everyone is worthy of love and respect.

7. Diet culture disproportionately affects women

Diet culture and sexism (the belief that women are inferior to men) are connected because if you believe you're inferior, you are more likely to do what others tell you to do and not listen to yourself. Without us having a sense of inferiority, diet culture *seriously* stops working. Imagine: you believe you are a worthwhile, lovable, amazing human who deserves respect just because you're alive, without conditions. Now imagine that you're told you need to lose weight so you can get a date/a raise/a husband/a different wardrobe. You won't fall for it.

8. Weight loss is part of accepting blame for fatphobia

There's a belief in the US that anyone, no matter who they are or where they started, can earn anything if they want it badly enough. We also believe that if someone doesn't get what they want (or need) it's because they didn't try hard enough. This is one of the biggest ideas that make up US culture. It's also one of the core ideas of diet culture. This sets up individuals to take on the blame for inequality. The truth is, individuals are not responsible for losing weight. Society is responsible for ending fatphobia.

9. Everyone is expected to be thin, and it's okay to be mean to people if they aren't

It's still considered totally normal to be openly mean to fat people in our culture. Fat people are socially punished, and the way we get treated is a lesson to people who are watching it happen. Again, if we return to history, it's kind of like the modern-day version of people getting locked into public restraining devices, where other people could throw a tomato at you for breaking a law. We don't detain people in the public square today, but we do give rewards to people who successfully conform, and punish people who don't. This shows up in dating, fashion, and school life.

write About It

Why do you think diet culture exists? Who benefits from it? Can you find stuff in your daily life that normalizes it?

Part Two

THOUGHTS ON COMMON BODY CONFUSIONS

7

Why Is My Family Always Talking About My Body?

You know what I used to hate more than anything? I'd be out shopping with my grandmother, and she would ask me if I was *sure* that something was gonna fit me. We were usually at the mall or at Target. I would pick up a dress or a sweater or a skirt that was super cute and that I loved—and that was totally my size—and I would show her.

She would wrinkle up her face and ask me: "Are you sure that's gonna fit?" No matter what I picked up, that's what she would say.

She and I have different ideas of what "fit" means. We are both plus-size. She prefers to dress more conservatively. She doesn't like showing off her stomach or her hips or her boobs. I, on the other hand, like body-con dresses, crop tops, and anything that's neon. I love to stand out. She doesn't.

When she was asking "Are you sure that's gonna fit?" it felt like she was really saying "I don't think you should wear that because I wouldn't wear that" or "I don't think you should wear that because you're too big to wear that."

I have a lot of memories of my grandmother—the woman who raised me—asking a lot of questions about my body.

I remember the first time I decided I wanted to sleep without a bra on. I was sixteen. My grandma has always worn a bra to bed, and she was totally horrified when I came to breakfast the next morning and she could see the outline of my nipples through my nightshirt. I remember that she accused my nipply breakfast look of being inappropriate, and she kind of shamed me by saying that the only reason a girl would choose not to wear a bra is if she had starting having sex. Weird theory.

I remember how embarrassed I felt, because I thought that she could see deep into my mind. Honestly, I thought it was more comfortable to sleep without a bra (and there's more than one reason someone stops wearing a tight undergarment to sleep), but it was also true that I had begun having phone sex with my boyfriend.

I was so scared that she was psychic. I was so scared that I was a bad person because I had a sexuality. In fact, I was experimenting with talking about my sexual desires in a safe way with a person I liked a lot and trusted.

I have tons of memories of people in my family talking about how I was too big or not pretty enough. They talked about how I looked older than I was because I was bigger than my cousins. My brother, on the other hand, was always getting comments about how he was too small for his age. So I guess it's safe to say that everyone has an opinion, and sometimes our family feels like they have an extra-special gold-plated permission slip that they can use whenever they want to pass judgment on us.

Sometimes it feels like people think they have the right to talk about you as if you weren't there.

Especially if you are perceived as a kid. Adults sometimes seem to think that kids can't understand them or hear them. PSA: I can hear you when you talk about me in front of my face.

Let me be clear: it's not cool for people to talk about your body or judge you. Your body is yours, and you have the right to do what you want with it—you have the right to dress the way you like, eat the way you like, grow out your eyebrows if you like, or wear a random giraffe-print scarf every day for a month if you like.

Let's get to the root of why people do stuff that hurts or anger us. Most of the time, our family comments on our body for a combination of reasons. None of these reasons, by the way, means it's okay for them to comment on your clothes or your body.

1. They're afraid that if we stand out something bad will happen to us

Maybe they have trauma that they haven't dealt with around this. It's helpful for family members we trust to give us their guidance on situations that might be *physically* dangerous, but it's not helpful for family members to try to control how others perceive us. Ironically, suppressing our real selves, trying to change our bodies, or hiding our true self-expression is often more dangerous to us and the people we love than just being our truest, brightest selves.

Unfortunately, when our family tries to protect us from getting hurt by asking us to change or commenting on our bodies, they are often the ones who are hurting us. We begin to lose trust and feel uncomfortable around them. We might feel rage or hurt. Those things are normal when someone is talking negatively about you.

2. They have judgments about their own bodies or the world that they are projecting onto us

Projection is when someone has a feeling that they are uncomfortable with, so they say that it's you who has that problem. For instance, someone is ashamed of their belly, but instead of admitting that their shame is theirs, they might talk negatively about how you look when you wear a crop top. Or maybe someone believes that women aren't supposed to wear short shorts, and instead of admitting that that is just one person's opinion, they use hurtful words to describe girls who don't believe the same thing.

3. They are being inappropriate and controlling

Sometimes our families feel like they own us and can do whatever they want to us. This is a myth, and it's hurtful. This belief often leads to actual physical or emotional abuse. I actually had to stop talking to my family in 2016 because of past experiences of them being controlling and abusive that they weren't willing to admit to.

When someone is coming for you, it's normal to be defensive; it's normal to be mad; it's normal to be hurt. Your feelings matter. You matter.

It is not okay for older people to project their expectations or opinions onto you. A lot of the time, because we don't want to rock the boat or be "disrespectful," our family gets a pass on all of their weird behaviors, and we feel disempowered to set boundaries or defend ourselves.

Sometimes in our families there are really strict and old-school ideas around what "respect" looks like. Like the idea that you have to respect your elders even if they're touching you inappropriately or talking about you in a way that makes you feel uncomfortable or angry.

This is not respect. This is submission. Submission doesn't really help anyone, but it really, super definitely doesn't help people who have less power in our families—like girls.

I remember all the times that people told me to be the bigger person or to turn the other cheek. Sometimes they would tell me that someone who was saying something hurtful was too old to change their ways and I just had to accept them the way they were.

Not true. No one is ever too old to change their ways. Fact: People can choose to be more kind and mindful until the day they die.

Even though it didn't feel good to swallow hurtful statements from others, I did it because I believed all the stuff that I was being told by people who were older than me.

Sometimes a tradition needs to be broken.

I want to talk a little bit about a tradition in my family that I helped to break. Like I said, I was raised by my grandparents. They were born in Mexico before 1950. They grew up with certain ideas about what a woman is and what a man is, and how men are allowed to treat women. Both of them also had complicated families. My grandmother was illegally taken out of school when she was in third grade and forced to work for her older sister, helping her run a restaurant and take care of her kids for no pay. My grandmother doesn't know how to read very well and doesn't feel comfortable with a lot of math. As a result of her childhood, she is very passive and doesn't defend herself often. That's the way she learned to deal with things and survive.

My grandfather was raised by a violent alcoholic who physically abused him when he was a child. He grew up dealing with everything by expressing anger, because anger was one of the only acceptable emotions for boys and men. Like in many alcoholic families, he was also expected to grow up really fast.

In addition, when my grandparents moved to the United States they experienced a lot of racism and xenophobia (fear of immigrants) because they spoke differently than white people and had darker skin.

As a result of all these things, there's a lot of trauma in my family. I grew up feeling afraid of my grandfather's temper, and frustrated that my grandmother never stood up to him. One time we were heading to Thanksgiving with my grandmother's extended family. My grandmother and grandfather got in a big fight in the car. He was screaming and she was crying. I was so scared and upset. I felt trapped and started to panic.

When we arrived at the place where we were having dinner, I was shaking. My grandmother and grandfather expected me to pretend as though nothing had happened, go inside, smile, and eat dinner.

But I just couldn't do it.

I called my boyfriend and told him what had happened, and he helped me get out of there. He encouraged me to speak up and tell my grandparents how much their behavior was hurting me.

When everyone got home that night, my grandmother was very angry at me. She accused me of ruining the meal. Instead of holding my grandfather accountable for his rage, she was worried that I had made her look bad in front of her extended family.

I asked them both to sit down, and I told them exactly how sad and scared I had been in the car. I asked my grandfather to stop doing this, and I told them that if it didn't stop that I would not be coming to Thanksgiving again.

I was a little older than you are—about twenty-five—when I did this. I had enough money to take a bus home and buy myself dinner. I lived away from my family in my own apartment. I had a cell phone, so I could call my boyfriend. Not everyone has that stuff, but all of us have a voice and the right to name our needs and feel safe.

At the end of the day, I broke a tradition—I refused to be silent about my grandfather's rage. I refused to act like everything was okay and cover it up. I set a clear boundary. It was scary, but it needed to happen. Breaking that tradition didn't just help me, it helped to show my grandparents that their behavior was part of a cycle of violence that had started a long time ago.

I know that my Thanksgiving story might seem totally disconnected from the idea of radical body positivity, but the truth is that your body is not just what's on the outside; it's also what's on the inside.

Sometimes when we are talking about our families and our bodies, it's not just about someone calling you a name or telling you that you don't look right or commenting on your body hair, your haircut, or your gender presentation. Sometimes we are also talking about feelings that live in your body. The way you feel affects your body. Whether or not you feel safe affects your immune system, your desires, your appetite, your goals, your ability to concentrate, and even your heart rate.

Remember: you have the right to set boundaries and communicate with your family around what you need to feel safe in your body.

One of my favorite tools for dealing with complicated communication is scriptwriting. Usually when we think of writing scripts we think of movies and television. Actually, a script can be any piece of writing that you can memorize and use so you don't have to make things up in the moment. Have you ever noticed that it's super hard to talk about your feelings when you're in the middle of being really mad or hurt? That's normal, and writing something ahead of time—when you're calm—can be really helpful for expressing your emotions.

This tool requires that you sit down with a piece of paper or your journal and write out the things that you want to say to family members (or anyone really) when you feel like your body is under attack.

> Remember: you have the right to set boundaries and communicate with your family around what you need to feel safe in your body.

It might be something simple like, "My body is my business." Or you could be more vulnerable, like, "When you say things about my body it makes me feel hurt and defensive, and I'm asking you to stop." If often helps to have a follow-up comment too, in case they don't respect your boundary. In the example of my grandmother, I might say: "If you don't stop commenting on how my clothes fit, then I will not be able to go shopping with you anymore."

It also may look like what happened when I talked to my grand-parents. It might look like talking about very old behaviors that started a long time ago, way before you were on this planet. The thing about family and family behavior is that most people just repeat whatever they saw their parents do. That's how things get passed on over and over and over again.

If you were not raised with the permission to self-advocate and set boundaries, you might be interrupting a super-old pattern. Some people talk about inheritances, like a piece of property, or a really nice pair of earrings, or your great-grandmother's silverware, or your weird auntie's salt and pepper shaker collection.

Behaviors and ideas are inheritances as well. We almost never talk about those. But they are just as real as the silverware or the salt and pepper collection. They get passed on from generation to generation.

The amazing thing about you is that you can decide which inheri-tances you want to keep and which ones you don't. You can decide which ones you want to change and improve and which ones need to go. You can use your intuition and talk to your friends about which inheritances make you feel good and safe, and you can add new ideas and behaviors for future generations to inherit.

write About It

What are the things your family does well when they communicate with you? What are things you'd like them to stop doing? What new traditions do you want the people who come after you to inherit? What's an old tradition you don't want to pass on?

8

Why Isn't Confidence Enough?

One time I spent $14.95 on a book that was supposed to teach me the secret to being irresistible to boys.

I had a really big crush on my classmate Ashneil. He had a great face. He was the fastest runner. He had the best turtlenecks. He was best friends with Joey, who was, like, so stone-cold cool. Looking back on it now, Ashneil was what you might call a total dirtbag. He only liked skinny girls and he was really mean to me. But I loved him. I thought it was totally normal that he hated me. Everyone hated me because I was fat, so Ashneil's hate didn't stand out. I thought it was my fault that he was mean to me, so I was able to forgive him again and again, no matter what he said. One time he even punched me in the arm and I convinced myself that I deserved it.

I believed that once I became thin (which never happened) his abusive behavior would stop and I would become his dream girl. And he would be my dream man.

I fantasized about us getting married and having babies and walking around hand in hand, showing everybody how cute we were in our matching turtlenecks. I dreamed of helping him pick out his favorite socks. I dreamed of giving him shoulder massages when he came home from school stressed out.

Okay, so most of these dreams were pretty sexist. Like, I don't need to help a grown man pick out his own socks, and men can use their income advantage over women to pay someone to massage them when they are stressed out.

But back to the book. The $15 secret? Confidence.

The book said that confidence would make me irresistible. My interpretation: it would make me Ashneil's girlfriend overnight.

The little book guided me through how to walk like I was confident and talk like I was confident. It guaranteed me that once I did all these steps, the man of my dreams would be begging for my phone number.

I did all the steps, but guess what? They didn't work! It turns out that I was still living in a culture that oppressed me because of my size, gender, and race (confidence can't cure oppression, unfortunately), and Ashneil was still super rude to me. I never became skinny, but I did stop having crushes on jerks. It turns out it's better to change who you have crushes on than trying to change yourself. New rule: people who punch people and verbally abuse them are not good crush material.

As I got older and went to college and then got a job, I saw the same thing over and over. A lot of people try to sell "confidence" to women as the secret to an amazing life—the partner of their dreams, the perfect job, or the house they see on those shows about perfect houses. The problem is, confidence can't exactly do all that stuff.

Confidence also can't solve big cultural problems, like sexism, racism, homophobia, and fatphobia.

Confidence is supposed to be the antidote to dealing with the stuff that happens because of cultural unfairness, like in the example with my crush. I thought confidence could make Ashneil love me, when I really needed to be focusing on the facts: 1. I deserve love because I'm a human; 2. My crush had super-oppressive ideas about the "right" kind of girl; and 3. The hateful behavior I was experiencing because of my body was part of oppression.

Sometimes confidence is sold to women as a way for us to become more appealing to men. The idea is that men love an "independent woman" because she's super busy and she has an amazing job; she doesn't put up with her man's ridiculous behavior (except she totally does); and then he writes a song about her afterward, praising her for sticking around while he threw a match on her life and burned it down in a massive trash fire.

In many of the examples of this independent superwoman, the reward for being independent is that she is loved by a man.

There is every kind of thing wrong with all of this.

It's great when someone writes a song about you, but not when they write a song praising you for taking all of their abusive garbage.

It's great when someone admires you because you have an amazing job, but it's not great when someone exploits you and takes advantage of your financial independence.

It's not okay to expect women to do a lot of extra work to get the attention of a man, because this perpetuates the myth that women are worth less than men and have to make up for the deficit by being extra amazing.

The thing I hate most about the confidence conversation is that sometimes confidence is a way of throwing the responsibility for oppression into the lap of the people who are experiencing it the most.

A lot of girls and women of color feel pressure to look tough or act strong all the time. That is part of our experience of racism and sexism.

Sometimes we get that pressure from our families, friends, and the representations of women of color in movies and on shows. We are encouraged to act like we are total badasses, when deep down maybe we actually don't feel so great; maybe we are tired of being so strong all the time. Sometimes looking confident—talking a certain way or acting a certain way—isn't the same as taking care of ourselves, setting boundaries, healing our heartaches, and making good decisions that truly benefit the collective (our friends, chosen family, and community). Sometimes girls and women of color are encouraged to use confidence like it's a coat of armor—like what a knight or warrior would wear into battle. Sometimes we need that armor to make it through a messed-up culture. But we also need to be able to take that armor off when we're with people we trust and when we're alone. We need to be able to recognize that it's armor, and that underneath there's a soft, kind, squishy human made of flesh and bones, with hopes and dreams and vulnerabilities.

Confidence isn't a bad thing, but you deserve more than that.

I am all for pushing your shoulders back and holding your head up high, but let's go past confidence, and talk about something far more powerful: self-love.

Self-love isn't about finding a partner or impressing other people; it's not about acting tough or wearing armor.

Self-love is about recognizing and accepting that you are precious and valuable—unconditionally—and creating a life that honors that truth. The word "unconditional" means absolute, unlimited, and not requiring anything in exchange. It means that no one can take it from you. It means that even when you forget it, it's still true. It means that you will always deserve this and it will always be yours no matter what: no matter what you can or cannot do, no matter how big or small your

> Self-love is about recognizing and accepting that you are precious and valuable

body is, no matter how much money you have, no matter whether you've got braces or acne, no matter what anyone says, no matter if you wear glasses or have a lisp or are bad at math, no matter what your hair looks like, no matter if everything you own is from a thrift store, no matter if you're dark or light, no matter if you have a lot of people crushing on you or not.

What if I told you that you are precious beyond belief—unconditionally?

What if I told you that you are valuable—unconditionally?

What if I told you that there's no one like you?

What if I told you that you don't have to earn love and acceptance, because you are already always worthy of love and acceptance—even if you feel like you're not getting it right now?

What if I told you that no matter what, you are a good and worthwhile person—unconditionally?

If a random stranger had told me in middle school or high school that I was valuable and perfect just the way I was, I would probably have laughed in their face and presumed that they were totally delusional or living on a planet called Not-Real-Life-Landia.

I would have asked them if they'd ever had to sit behind the jerk who made fun of their outfit every day. I would have asked them if they'd ever met my teacher, who called people dumb. I would have asked them if they'd ever seen a movie.

Yes, Girl. I lived the saddest life. It's not easy being the fat brown girl with acne who eats tuna sandwiches wrapped in foil. I was that girl. Now here I am, writing a book from my apartment in San Francisco, burning a Dolly Parton candle, about to fly to New York for Fashion Week.

I know, I know. I know that what I'm suggesting is a wild, radical idea, but I also know that it's true.

It's not just jocks and cheerleaders who deserve respect and dignity, and whose bodies are valuable. We don't have to aspire to be a jock or a cheerleader.

We can just be ourselves and expect other people to catch up to the Self-Love Train.

A lot of times we equate confidence with having a certain kind of body, especially if we are a girl. In our culture women and girls are taught that we can trade our bodies for love and for admiration.

The truth is, every body is a good body. The truth is, no one should be treated differently because of their gender or ability or hair texture or skin tone or what their family can afford to buy them. We get all kinds of cultural messages that tell us that we have to look better and be better and have more money. But the truth is, you are enough. Right now.

You were born already enough, you are currently enough, and you always will be enough.

Everything in the culture is telling you that I'm wrong, I know. I'm sure you feel pressure to just go along with whatever everyone else says is normal, no matter how it makes you feel. I'm sure you get told by other people that you are the one who needs to change so you can meet others' expectations. But consider for one solid second why the culture teaches us that. Because self-love is super radical. When we love ourselves, we stand up for ourselves, we listen to our bodies, we recognize our humanity, and we don't settle for less. These acts legit disrupt history.

This is what power looks like. You have that power inside you. You've just gotta activate it.

Write About It

How would your behaviors, thoughts, and actions change if you truly believed that you were precious, valuable, and unconditionally a good person who deserved love? What do you need, beyond confidence, to feel good about yourself and your body?

9

What Do I Say to Trolls?

Some people call them bullies or jerks. Other people call them trolls. I call them abusers, because that's what they are. A troll/bully/jerk/abuser uses words and behaviors to undercut another person's self-esteem because they want to control them.

If you're anything like I was in high school, you blame yourself when people are jerks to you. This is really common when you've experienced oppression, like racism, sexism, or fatphobia.

Here's an important mind-shift I want you to try thinking about next time someone is emotionally abusive:

People who don't like me because of my body are trolls. Trolling is abuse. There's nothing wrong with my body. When someone chooses to abuse me, they are wrong and should change their behavior. I don't need to change my body to make abusers feel comfortable.

One day, I was heading home on the train, and a woman near where I was standing leaned over and told her boyfriend in a loud whisper that I was too fat to wear what I had on—a short dress with tights and boots. I thought about ignoring her, but that day I realized

I needed to speak up—not just for me, but for every person who has had to endure a comment like that.

I gave her a big slice of my special Shameless Fat Girl Pie. I walked right up to her and told her that I could wear whatever I wanted to wear and that she didn't need to feel threatened by my amazing outfit. I also informed her that I looked really good, actually. And then I sat down right next to her. We sat there in (yes, awkward) silence for forty-five minutes, from downtown San Francisco all the way to the Pacific Ocean, the end of the line.

I wish I could wave a magic wand and protect you from jerks forever and ever. Unfortunately, no one has that power. But here's a million-dollar secret: trolls act out because they are afraid that something will change and they'll have less power over others. And yup, that's terrible. You can't change them. You can't spend your precious time giving them troll rehab. Your only job is to keep yourself far away and safe from them. The best thing you can do for them and yourself is to learn to stand up for yourself, create boundaries, and have a plan of action when you're hurt by others' words or behavior.

Sometimes trolling shows up online. Sometimes it shows up IRL. Sometimes it comes from people we don't like. Sometimes it comes from people who are in our friend circle. Sometimes it's extremely obvious, because the troll is telling you to your face that they're a troll. Sometimes it's not, and you can feel it in the way they say things or how they look at you. Again: trust your gut!

I'm a fat brown lady who wears tight clothes on the internet. So I know all kinds of trolls.

Some trolls attack my looks, saying that I'm a feminist or a fat activist only because I'm not beautiful. Some trolls attack my health, saying that I'm going to die young because of my weight (even though research shows that fat people live as long as thin people, and the leading reason that fat people have more health problems is because of the stress of being attacked constantly for being fat). Some trolls attack my body, saying that my fatness makes me disgusting. Some trolls attack my safety, threatening to harm me. Some trolls attack my character, saying that I'm not a good enough person to be doing the work I do. Some trolls attack my sanity, saying that I'm clearly not stable because patriarchy isn't a real thing. Some trolls attack my talents, saying I'm not a good writer. Some trolls attack my intelligence, telling me I'm stupid. Some trolls attack my gender, saying that if I had a husband I wouldn't have time to be doing activism. And some trolls are low-key and use under-the-radar tactics, like someone who never comments on anything good I do or a happy moment in my life, but is *always* there lurking and waiting to criticize when I mess up. (I'm a human, so making mistakes is inevitable.)

In my daily life I deal with trolls who have opinions about what I'm wearing, who I'm on a date with, or what I'm eating.

When it comes to women's bodies, the culture is kind of like a big old troll.

It trolls women through ads, movies, magazines, and individuals who have bought into harmful, bigoted attitudes. Many people hide behind the anonymity of the internet in order to say hurtful, judgmental, and small-minded things.

The good news is that feminists have come up with a whole lot of tools for how to deal with these trolls. I'd like to share some.

So you got trolled. Here are some steps to deal with it.

Step 1: Recognize that you have the right to live a life free from hateful speech and behavior. You do not deserve to be treated poorly, no matter what you look like, what your gender presentation is, or how much money you have.

Step 2: Check in with your emotions. Are you angry? Are you sad? Let yourself really *feel* the emotion. Maybe you don't feel comfortable looking vulnerable in front of other people right away, but as soon as you're able to, take some time to let yourself feel bummed out. Even though it may really suck, letting yourself be mad or sad are important parts of being human. When we don't let ourselves feel feelings, they get stuck in our bodies and show up as resentment or rage.

Step 3: Check in with your self-care tool kit. What helps you feel better? Do you love to journal? Do you love to grab your phone and take weird photographs of your feet (I do) or trees? Do you have a favorite candle that smells super good that you can light? Do you have a tiny cactus you can talk to (I do)? Do you have a favorite piece of clothing you can bust out when you're feeling heartbroken? Do you have a favorite pair of comfy pajamas that you can put on? (I personally love wearing fuzzy socks when I am feeling bummed out. It's like two teddy bears hugging my feet while I feel all the feelings.) Do you have a friend who is really good at listening to, supporting, and affirming you? Do you have a favorite book that makes you feel comforted? Do you love to draw? Whatever is in your tool kit, now's the time to take it out.

Step 4: Set boundaries. Warning: setting boundaries often feels uncomfortable at first. That's normal. What are some simple things you can say to the troll that lets them know that their words aren't acceptable? Can you opt out of engaging with them, even a little? I'll share something from my tool kit: when someone in my social circle is trolling me and isn't respecting my boundaries, I opt out of gatherings that include them, or I refuse to spend quality time with them.

Sometimes the best thing to do with a troll is to ignore them (especially if they're an internet troll), but it's important to know that you absolutely have the right to defend your body in the face of harassment. The secret, gold-star move is to set boundaries quickly, without getting too engaged.

On the next page are some quick and easy things to say to a troll.

Stuff to say to trolls

1. My body is my business

2. My body; my rules

3. You don't get to talk to me like that

4. I know my body best

5. I didn't ask for your opinion

6. I don't need to be ashamed of my body; you need to be ashamed of being a bigot

7. I represent a threat to the status quo—what do you represent?

8. I understand that the idea that I love myself is foreign to you, but I don't have time to explain body-positive feminism right this second

Here are some other tools that are useful for internet trolls:

1. Make your social media accounts private

2. Be intentional about who you follow

3. Make a promise to yourself that you won't engage with trolls

Unfortunately, we don't live in a world where it's possible to prevent ourselves from being hurt. Being hurt is part of being human.

I know my body best

Yes, trolls live on the internet, but they also live in our classrooms and sometimes even at home with us. Sometimes they are our teachers, neighbors, or family members. It's important to remember that anyone who says something hurtful to you is doing something wrong and bad. They are doing something that is abusive. When someone calls you a name, it is never your fault. When someone decides to be hurtful, it is their responsibility to be better, not your job to change.

Write About It

What would you add to your list of stuff to say to trolls? What's in your self-care tool kit?

10

I'm Tired of Hating Myself...So How Do I Love Myself?

For a long time I used to wake up every day with the same thought: I hate this body. As a fat girl of color, I was taught that my body didn't deserve love—that I didn't deserve to love myself.

When I was introduced to feminism, anti-racism, and fat activism, I learned about how sexism, racism, and fatphobia had taught me to hate my body. I read about the history of these things and got super mad about all of it. Anger is important! Don't be afraid of getting angry.

The new friends I met through my political activism helped me learn how to love my body. I want to share with you some of the stuff they taught me.

Let's start with some basics: our culture teaches women and girls of color to hate and feel ashamed of our bodies.

In our culture most women—regardless of size, race, ability, or income—don't like their bodies and think something is super wrong with them.[19] The reason? Sexism. When you are a person of color, there is an extra layer of racism that creates shame around our skin, our hair, our body shape, or the way we talk. If you have other qualities that are marginalized—like you're queer, trans, fat, or disabled—those are extra layers on top of race and gender.

The evidence of all of this exists in our daily lives. Most of the models, actors, and people we see portrayed as heroes are white, able-bodied, thin, cisgender people. Most US presidents have been white men. Most superheroes are white. Almost every person who's won an Academy Award for best actress is white. Women of color make less money than white women at work.

A lot of women of color experience something called "internalized racism." When something is internalized, that means it's inside of you—hanging out in your subconscious.

Don't freak out! Every single person, regardless of how privileged they are, experiences internalization around *something*. It's good to know it's there, because it can help you understand what motivates certain thoughts or behaviors. Just because you know it's there doesn't mean you have to let it run your life.

You can build the life you want to live, even while dealing with and healing from internalized racism.

Internalized racism affects how you see the world, who you look up to, who you have crushes on, who you want to get close to, and who you envision dating. This might look like feeling ashamed of having darker skin or a different body shape than the white bodies we see all the time. It may look like having crushes only on white people. It may look like wanting to have straighter hair or lighter eyes. It may also mean wanting to talk a certain way.

I want to tell you about one way that internalized racism showed up in my life.

In second grade I decided that I wanted to start talking like my teacher, Mrs. Moore. She was a beautiful, tall, elegant white woman—like the kind I had seen on TV that everyone loved. I had never met one of these kinds of women in real life. Until then I had talked like my grandma, who has a Mexican accent. Until I met Mrs. Moore, my grandma had been my feminine role model.

So I emulated Mrs. Moore. My admiration and respect for her—in addition to the fact that I had learned that white women were better than people like me or my grandmother—made me want to be like her. Because our country has a long history of racism, it was almost inevitable that the people I would look up to would be white people. These are the people I was seeing in positions of authority on television, in movies, in cartoons, and in magazines. Everyone who was good, smart, beautiful, brave, or heroic on TV was a white person. Who doesn't want to be good and smart and beautiful and brave and heroic?

Because I am also fat, I was taught through abusive behavior (aka bullying or trolling), cultural messages, and media portrayals that fat people are lazy, stupid, and undesirable. Most of the time thin people, by contrast, are portrayed as ambitious, attractive, and sexy.

I learned that dieting was something I was expected to do. Everyone told me it was for my own health and happiness, but I didn't feel healthy or happy. I felt anxious, depressed, and hungry. Dieting was harming me. Sometimes I wouldn't eat enough and I'd get dizzy or nauseous. At one point I was eating so little that I just started falling asleep all the time, because my body didn't have enough calories to keep me awake. No matter what I did, as long as it looked like I was losing weight, everyone told me I was doing a good job.

Even my family doctor congratulated me after I had practically starved myself for an entire summer. Now that I'm older, I know that was wrong. My doctor was wrong. The people who were encouraging me to diet were wrong. There was nothing wrong with my body. I was just naturally bigger than other people, and I was the right size for me.

As a result of fatphobia—the cultural belief that fat people are inferior and should do everything in their power to become thin people—many fat people aren't eating enough food for their bodies. Many people who diet think they are just "watching what they eat," but actually they may have disordered eating.

I was one of those people. The National Eating Disorders Association reports that 35 percent of "normal dieters" progress to nonstop dieting and that 20–25 percent of those individuals develop eating disorders.[20]

After the combined efforts of television, movies, advertising, and internet trolls, we are lucky if we enter adulthood without a serious case of super-low self-esteem. One of the hardest things I've learned is that this isn't an accident. Big companies know that they can get us to buy a lot of products if they make us feel like something is wrong with us, like I told you about in Chapter 2. Our culture has made a lot of money off of women of color's insecurities.

So it's no surprise that most women and girls of color don't like the way they look. The combined forces of sexism and racism leave us feeling like something is very wrong with us.

The feeling that something is wrong with you is part of disempowerment.

Disempowerment makes us feel like we don't have power, even though we have lots of it. It makes it harder for us to set boundaries, say no, take care of ourselves, put ourselves first, love our bodies, and celebrate exactly who we are. It is connected to who we date and are attracted to. It is connected to what kind of job we look for and what kind of ambitions we have.

I remember one time I was on a date with a white man. He made less money than I did and was younger than me, but the culture was built to accommodate him and make sure he succeeded. So he ended up giving me some career advice that changed my life.

I had been giving lectures here and there at different colleges, and on our first date he said, "You should be thinking about lecturing at Harvard."

Harvard?! It had literally never even occurred to me that I could shoot as high as Harvard. How did a broke white man have bigger dreams for me than I did?

The answer was simple: I wasn't raised to have the love for myself that this white dude was taught to have for himself, and that affected how valuable I thought I was and how much I felt I deserved.

Hating ourselves takes up a lot of energy and time. Imagine all the stuff you'd get done if you didn't feel self-conscious or worried about what other people think about you.

Imagine what your life would look like if you felt like you were totally perfect just the way you are, like there was nothing about yourself that you needed to change, and like you were capable of truly extraordinary things. What would be different?

Once I stopped spending all my time counting calories and worrying about whether my hair was straightened, I found I had a lot of time to develop better practices—practices that were not based on the fear that I wasn't pretty enough or good enough.

Self-love meant I had to change a lot of things about my everyday life. I had to stop dating people who judged how I ate or how I looked. I had to tell my friends that they couldn't talk about their bodies negatively in front of me. I had to stop looking at some of my favorite magazines, because all of the models were very thin and very light-skinned. I had to get rid of clothes that didn't fit me anymore. I had to throw away my scale. I had to start reading books that didn't shame people's bodies (harder to find than you might realize!). I started focusing on media that was made *by* women of color *for* women of color.

> Ask your friends and family to join you in no longer using body-shaming language

Self-love is—in my humble opinion—always worth it. Putting love into the world or into ourselves is always a positive thing that helps us, the planet, and humanity.

Hatred—whether it's hatred toward others or toward ourselves—will always lead to harm, abuse, and negative outcomes. Love is where all amazing things begin.

Forty quick things you can do to develop self-love

1. Unfollow social media accounts that make you feel bad about yourself

2. Don't read magazines that portray mostly only one kind of body

3. Make your own zine about body hair or body fat or how awesome dark skin is

4. Get rid of your "skinny" jeans

5. Talk to your friends about how they feel about their bodies

6. Ask your friends and family to join you in no longer using body-shaming language

7. Stop saying negative stuff about yourself

8. Stop dieting

9. Ask your friends if they'll read this book and then talk with you about it

10. Practice not calling food "good" or "bad"

11. Write yourself some cute, affirming sticky notes and put them on your mirror or in your locker

12. Take down any images you may have posted of "goal" bodies

13. Set boundaries with people who say hurtful stuff about you

14. Say out loud as often as possible: "I'm valuable and sacred"

15. Write a love letter to your body

16. Light a little candle, and for the entire time that it burns, think or write down nice things about yourself until it goes out

17. Wear clothes that make you feel comfortable

18. Don't date or have crushes on people who are homophobic, transphobic, fatphobic, or racist

19. Watch movies and shows that portray all kinds of people in empowering and positive ways

20. Make your own rules about what, when, and how people get to touch you

21. Say no when you mean no. Say yes when you mean yes.

22. Trust your body. Trust your gut. When something feels wrong, trust the feeling.

23. Listen to your emotions. If you're angry, be angry. If you're sad, be sad.

24. Remember that when someone comments negatively on your body, it's *never* your fault

25. Take a few minutes before or after school to sit down in a quiet place and just breathe deeply

26. Think about what you *really* want. Even if it doesn't seem possible right now, imagine it happening.

27. Speak up about bullying and hateful speech to your teachers and parents, until they take action

28. Take some extra time to do something that makes you feel special—like putting lotion on your feet or massaging oil into the ends of your hair

29. Make stuff! You can add salt to some water to make a curl-enhancing salt spray for your hair. You can add lavender essential oil to water to make a pillow spray. You can add coconut oil to coffee grounds to make a body scrub. You can add dried rose petals to regular tea to make it self-love tea.

30. Alter clothes you were planning to donate—like turn an old T-shirt into a crop top, or sew some colorful buttons onto your gloves or a scarf, or sew one of your identities into your fave socks (like "queer" or "feminist" or "melanated" or "gender-free")

31. Write a story in which you're the main focus, from the perspective of someone who admires you. My favorite: my neighbor has a crush on me, loves all my weird outfits, and dreams of the day when we go and get boba together.

32. Envision your body five, ten, fifteen, and twenty years from now, with roughly the same proportions. Not radically different-looking. What are you doing? What are you wearing? Write about your visions.

33. Come up with a secret thing that makes you feel like yourself or makes you feel grounded. Maybe it's a bracelet,

necklace, or earring, or a little drawing, or a note written in a secret language that you carry with you. My favorite is a rose quartz stone. Whenever life gets rough, touch that thing and remind yourself that you've got this.

34. Think about policies and rules in your life and advocate against discrimination against you and other women, queer people, people of color, and disabled people

35. Watch movies and social media with a critical lens. Notice who the main characters are and who the villains are, and ask yourself why. Notice how people of different races, sizes, and economic backgrounds are portrayed, and ask yourself why.

36. Experiment with different lengths of hair, growing out body hair, and how you dress

37. Focus on communicating what you want and need. If you're new to this, practice being assertive and clear first, rather than going straight to yelling at someone. :) If they don't listen, then you can move on to a different strategy.

38. Listen to music that makes you feel seen and heard

39. Talk to yourself the way you'd talk to someone you really love. That means no more insults or name-calling.

40. Recognize that it's okay to have bad days when you're really down on yourself. You didn't fail! Remind yourself that you didn't choose to learn crappy body ideals.

✏️
write About It

Add ten more things you want to see on this list.

Part Three

BE YOU, NOT WHAT SOMEONE ELSE THINKS YOU SHOULD BE

11

Your Body Does Amazing Stuff Every Single Day, Girl

A few years ago I was working on a book about fat women who had made the decision to stop dieting and start living their best lives at their current size. They each wrote a chapter in response to one question: "How did you learn to love your body in a culture that taught you to hate it?"

One of the first people I spoke to told me a story about how her belly had saved her life when she was in a bad car accident.

This person's name is Erin, and she's an artist who lives in Seattle. I remember we were sitting by a swimming pool wearing sunglasses, reclined in these big plastic chairs. I leaned forward as she explained.

When the accident happened, all she saw was a truck coming from the opposite direction, crossing the dividing line and into her lane. Her small car was totaled; it didn't even have airbags. She had to get pried out of the car by the jaws of life, and then a helicopter picked her up and took her to the hospital.

She was covered in cuts and bruises, but when the doctor came in to tell her the damage, he had some surprising news: she had absolutely no internal organ damage from this horrible accident. He told her that she was lucky she had extra weight, because it had prevented her from being seriously injured. She said, "It's pretty hard to hate your body after something like that."

I love that story, because it's the kind of story you never hear about. Erin is fat, and her body is looked down on in our culture right now, but that body actually saved her life. A thinner person probably wouldn't have made it out of that car crash with no damage, but Erin did. I have spoken to hundreds of women and heard lots of stories like that—a body part that they had hated actually helped them to do something important. We all should appreciate our bodies and the miraculous things that our bodies do all day every day, but unfortunately most of us don't.

You were taught—by media, cultural norms, and advertising—to look at your body and see what's wrong with it.

Maybe you feel like you're too short, too tall, or too skinny, that you have bad hair or bad skin, that you're too big or too dark or too light. I know all about those kinds of feelings. For a long time all I saw when I looked in the mirror were flaws.

Sexism plays into the way we are taught to think about our bodies. We are taught to think of what we look like first, because we live in a culture that deemphasizes what girls are capable of doing and focuses instead on what we look like. The good news: you don't have to worry about what others think about how you look.

It helps to focus on all the incredible things your body does. When you start to criticize yourself, it really helps to instead remember what your body *can* do.

Do you ever stop and think about all the amazing stuff your body is doing all the time, without you even having to think about it?

All day long, your heart beats. Whether you're asleep or awake, your heart pumps blood into your arms, legs, lungs, and brain. Every single day, your hair and nails grow just a little. You don't have to think about it. It just happens.

Your brain works together with your eyes to effortlessly read this book. Your eyes process information that your brain translates as colors, images, voices—without you even having to think about it.

Your ears can detect sounds; they can tell you if you're hearing a movie or your friend's laughter or your teacher's voice. They allow you to hear crickets at sunset. They help you know if a car is getting too close. They let you hear the beat of your favorite song.

Your skin is this huge, amazing organ that lets you feel sensations—the warmth of the sun, the cold of the ocean, the pleasure of a soft sweater, the way it feels to hold someone's hand, the texture of a flower petal, the sensation of rain, or the prick of a cactus.

Your tongue talks to your brain and lets you taste all the amazing stuff you've ever tasted: Cheetos, birthday cake, peanut butter, sushi, nachos, pizza, kimchi, chili, tacos, pupusas, ghost peppers. It lets you know when something tastes bad or is rotten.

Your brain processes language so people can talk to you and you can understand them. It stores your best memories. It works to help you recover from traumatic events. It learns and retains new information.

Your intuition lives in your body. Some people think it lives in the old, reptilian part of your brain. Others believe it lives deep in your stomach—that's why some people call it a "gut feeling." Whenever something just *feels right*—or wrong—that's your intuition telling you to listen.

Your stomach takes everything you eat and works with your intestines and other internal organs to turn that food into fuel that you can use to think, do homework, have fun, move around, and interact with others.

Your feet are made up of twenty-six connected bones that keep you upright, that move you around, that let you run, walk, play basketball, go bowling, and jump on your bed. They have more than 100 muscles and thousands of nerve endings that let you feel sand and grass.

At night, we fall asleep and we dream. Our dreams help us deal with things that are happening all around us during the daytime. Our dreams sometimes tell us if we have unconscious stuff we have to deal with. While we're sleeping, our body recovers and reenergizes. Have you ever had a cut or a scrape, fallen asleep, and found it was almost completely healed by the time you woke up?

Thanks, body.

Speaking of injuries, whenever you get hurt, your body jumps into action right away. Your brain gets a signal that something bad has happened. It tells you where the hurt is. If you have a cut, your body immediately starts a clotting reaction in order to close up the wound and create a scab. Scabs are kinda gross, but without scabs we would just bleed all over the place for a long time. If you hurt a muscle, your body immediately starts to try and heal it—the same with broken bones. That's why you have to make sure to set a bone straight right after you break it—because your body will start to heal it even if the bone isn't in the right place.

When's the last time you cried? Crying is your body's natural way of releasing emotions. I have a theory that we cry because water is how we move overwhelming emotions out of our bodies when they're more than we can handle. That's why I think it hurts when we hold back tears.

In addition to all this, we each have unique things that our bodies can do. Like, I can make a tongue taco, which I often bust out at parties if things get boring. I am super strong because I have a big body, and big bodies require that our muscles get buff. And my taste buds are really good at picking up certain flavors, for example if something has an herb like lavender in it.

I know for sure that your body can do unique things, but even if you can't think of any right now, you can always remember all the amazing things that every single body does all the time, like pumping blood, breathing, and using muscles to help you coordinate. In the moments when someone insults your body or you forget how truly amazing and magical your body is, all you have to do is slow down for a moment and listen to your body's miraculous ability to breathe without effort. Look down and wiggle your fingers, made possible by an intricate coordination of your brain and muscles.

Close your eyes and listen to what you're able to hear because you have ears that are connected to eardrums that allow you to detect a bird or a voice or a train and know what it is. Touch your skin and remember that this organ will be with you forever, allowing you to experience the most important sensations of your life. Remember that no matter what you look like—whether you have a disability, no matter your body size, your weight, your color, your gender, your sexuality, or your height, or whether you have an illness or not—you are 100 percent flawless.

write About It

What are three unique things your body can do?

12

Say No at Least once a Day

Growing up, I watched the women in my family—my mom and grandma—do way too much to make sure everyone else was comfortable.

My grandma cooked dinner for a family of six every night and—because in Mexican tradition women serve men and children—she also made sure she got everyone everything they asked for or needed during dinner.

If someone wanted ice for their soda, she'd get up and get it.

If someone needed ketchup for their fries, she'd get up and get it.

If my grandpa wanted seconds, she was the one who would get them.

If my brother wanted his food heated up in the middle of the meal, she'd put it in the microwave.

If I wanted to add parmesan to my spaghetti, she would make sure I had it.

My mom is bipolar, a mental illness that causes intense mood swings. Some days she'd be my idea of the best mom in the world, some days she'd be super angry and mean, and some days she wouldn't be able to get out of bed. On those days, she wouldn't be at the table, but when she wasn't in bed she'd be running around with my grandma during the meal too. Sometimes they wouldn't even sit down at all for dinner—one or both of them would just stand at the counter and eat between tasks. In addition to that, sometimes my grandfather would complain about the temperature of the food or say that it took too long to get it on the table.

My grandmother and mom probably did all this because they didn't feel like they could say no, but I wish they had.

Everyone deserves to be able to say no.

Because I grew up with it, I thought this was all totally normal behavior. I never questioned why my grandpa didn't get up to get anything or why he never washed the dishes. He worked outside of the house, and even though my grandma worked to clean the house and ran errands all day, she didn't get to clock out of work the way my grandpa did. He got to kick up his feet and relax the minute he came home, but my grandma didn't. Even though she'd been working hard all day to take me to school, get groceries, vacuum, cook, and clean, when my grandfather got home she had to get to work on making sure he felt like a king.

Feminists call this the "second shift": the work that women have had to do historically when their husbands got home from work and their kids got home from school—*after* they'd already worked all day.[21]

My grandpa worked an eight-hour shift, from 6:00 a.m. to 2:00 p.m. My grandma worked a fifteen-hour shift: from the time my grandpa woke up to the time we all went to bed.

As a kid, I never questioned how annoying or tiring—or maybe even hurtful—it must have been for my mom or grandma to do all that work. I just thought this was how things were: women run around and take care of everything, and men sit down and complain about how they're doing it wrong. (Not cool, men who do that.)

I'm lucky that my mom didn't believe that I had to be polite. When I was a little girl, older people would try to hold me or touch me, and if I said I didn't want to, she'd respect that and speak up for me. She empowered me to say "no" at a young age, but then as I got older I gave into the gender expectations of accommodating others.

People don't like it when girls and women say no to stuff. Girls are expected to be "nice" to their family members and sometimes strangers. Sometimes being nice comes at a big cost to us.

I want to tell you that when someone touches you without your permission or expects you to do something you don't want to do, you actually don't need to be nice. You need to take care of yourself and keep yourself safe.

Saying no is part of keeping your mind, body, and emotions safe.

"No" is a very powerful little word. It's one of my favorites. It's fun to say, and it's a required part of any radical, body-positive babe's tool kit. If you're not used to saying no, then I recommend starting with saying no once a day.

"No" wasn't a serious part of my vocabulary until I was, like, twenty-one. It totally changed my life in the best way. I'm kind of jealous that you get to learn this before I did, but I'm glad I get to be the one who tells you about it.

> Saying no is part of keeping your mind, body, and emotions safe.

I learned about the power of no from my friends in college. They were feminists and they encouraged me to begin checking in with my body and my desire before I agreed to do things.

When I learned that I had the right to say no, I started using that power frequently.

I started saying no to my grandpa's misogyny.

I started saying no to people who asked to borrow money and never paid it back.

I started saying no to people who wanted to tell me I shouldn't be wearing what I wanted.

I started saying no to people who used racist words.

I started saying no to my classmates who wanted me to do more work than them.

I started saying no to random people on the street talking about my body.

I started saying no to people who wanted to date me but never asked me any questions about myself.

I started saying no when I was too tired to spend time with my friends (even though I loved spending time with them).

The word "no" helped me to set boundaries and gave me an opportunity to listen to my body. If we pay attention, our bodies are constantly sending us messages, letting us know what we like and what we don't like.

Like, when I'm excited about something, my eyes open a little bit more, I smile, my toes and fingers wiggle a little bit, and I feel like the energy in my body is moving up through me—from my belly to my head. When I'm not into something, I find that my eyes narrow a little bit, my body slumps a little, and I feel like the energy in my body is moving downward—from my head to my belly. Sometimes, if I really don't like something I will feel my stomach drop a little, like I'm on a roller coaster. Or I will find myself making excuses or looking for ways to delay doing the thing I don't want to do.

Sometimes our body is saying no, but we ignore our body and say yes to things because we want to be nice or we want to be polite. We need to stop ignoring our bodies and say yes only when we mean yes. People who really love and respect us will understand why we say no. They won't make us feel bad about it.

Sometimes people don't realize that they're asking too much of us, and sometimes people don't really care about how something makes us feel because they care only about their needs. They just expect their needs to be met by someone else.

Sometimes we really want to do something, but we just don't have the time, energy, or resources to do it. No matter what the reason, you always have the right to say no. "No" is one of the things in your tool kit that helps you make sure that you are taking care of your physical and emotional needs.

You have a limited amount of energy, time, and resources to share. It's important to make sure that at least half of that stuff is going toward taking care of yourself.

Because of sexism, girls and women have been taught that saying no is rude and selfish and that we should give away all of our energy, time, and resources. The truth is, it's not rude *or* selfish to take care of yourself, set boundaries, and tell people that you have limits. You deserve that! Everyone has limits and needs care. You're not a bad person for saying no to requests that don't feel good in your body, or requests that you don't have the energy, time, or desire to do.

It takes a while for people to catch up if you've never said no to them before, but they will. I promise. If they don't, that means they don't have it in them to take care of you, or they're just not awesome people. Don't sweat not-awesome people when they leave your life. It might hurt at first, but you'll be okay, and they might come back when they're ready to respect your needs.

write About It

How does it feel in your body when you're excited to say yes to something? How does it feel in your body when you're not excited and want to say no to something? What are three things that you'd like to start saying no to?

13

Never, Ever Skip Lunch (or Breakfast or Dinner)

I want to tell you a story about a sad time in my life when I skipped a lot of lunches, breakfasts, and dinners. It happened when I was eleven. I didn't know about all the research that says that skipping meals is bad for people. I didn't know about radical body positivity or fat activism. I thought something was wrong with me and my body, and everyone told me that I should do whatever I had to do to change my body. They said the best way to change my body was to eat less food.

The people around me were wrong for telling me I needed to change my body, and they were wrong to encourage me to eat less than I wanted and needed, but I didn't know that at the time.

This story happened during the summer between fifth and sixth grades. I decided I was really, really going to finally become thin. Every magazine I saw at the grocery store told me that losing weight was a good goal and an easy goal. I would stay up late and watch infomercials about exercise and diet pills. Even though I had been trying to be thin for a long time and it seemed impossible, I was sure that the problem was my inability to do it *the right way*.

I had been on diets before, but this time I was ready to make sixth grade the best year of my life. I was sure that the key to this was eating way, way less than I ever had before. The secret to a hot boyfriend, amazing outfits, and the end of being treated like trash was to take my regular dieting to the next level. I needed results, and I needed them fast.

In the days leading up to summer, I had begun daydreaming about what my sixth-grade life was going to look like.

I imagined the scene over and over again. It was like a movie. My alarm clock would go off on the first day of sixth grade and I'd wake up. The sun would come in through my curtains and shine down on my face. As my eyes slowly opened, I'd realize that this was my special day. The camera would zoom in on me smiling as I pushed the covers off my bed, looked at myself in the mirror, and bit my lip as I headed to the bathroom. I'd jump on the scale and find that the number was exactly my goal weight. Wow! The feeling of being thin would wash over my body and I'd reach into my closet—past all my old clothes, which were too big for me now—and pull out...

Are you ready?

...black spandex pants and a tiny black tube top.

I would slip on some black wedge sandals, do my hair, and then begin the three-block walk to school—out the door, through the gate, turn left, walk past the neighbor with the white Labrador, past the lady who always watered the lawn in her pink muumuu, past the mailbox. Then I would begin my descent down the concrete walkway that led straight to the schoolyard. The second my wedge heel hit the grass, music would begin to play. It was the music that played in all the transformation movies I'd seen about women going from "not" to "hot." Like a pop song with strong vocals that is kind of empowering.

The song would signal that all the kids in the schoolyard (including Ashneil, my dream man and eternal crush) would need to look back and see me—in slow motion—as I tossed my hair back over my bare shoulder.

The grass would transition into the blacktop, and that's when things would get super interesting. I'd jump on the horizontal bar and proceed to do a bunch of gymnastic-level twirling. (Now that I was thin, I'd just be able to do that kind of stuff, even though I had never been trained in gymnastics.) I'd spin and everyone would *ooh* and *aah*, and then I'd end by dismounting onto my feet. Then I'd walk straight into Ashneil's arms and we'd kiss—without ever talking about all the mean stuff he'd said and done to me when I was fat, because that was in the past now. He'd recognize that I was the girl of his dreams and we'd live happily ever after.

The minute that bell rang on the last day of fifth grade, the countdown began. I had three months to become the hottest girl at school, get my dream dude, become popular, and then begin the life that would totally make me the perfect wife and mother after we graduated from high school. I had already made a plan as to how to achieve all this: all I needed to do was eat almost nothing.

I truly believed that if I could just stop eating, all my dreams could come true.

I decided on lettuce and toast with an occasional dab of barbecue sauce. I would also need to exercise a lot—like two or maybe three hours a day. I had found an exercise routine on VHS for this. It was sixty minutes long. Perfect.

That summer was brutal. Instead of playing, I was working out. Instead of eating ice cream at the pool, I was eating the saddest version of a sandwich, *kinda*. But the weeks went on, and before long it was the end of summer. I had lost weight and gone down in clothes size. My family said I looked great. Even my doctor told me to keep up the good work.

I was proud, but the first day of school came and my special moment on the playground never happened. Even though I had basically starved myself, it just wasn't enough. I didn't get my dream boy. I didn't become the hottest girl at school. But instead of giving up on diets or meal-skipping, I was determined to keep trying.

When I was eighteen, I attempted a more drastic version of my sixth-grade summer diet. I decided I was going to try to eat nothing—maybe a spoonful of food a day. It didn't take long before I got super sick. I was constantly dizzy and nauseous. I had to take naps all the time because I was so tired. I didn't understand that the reason I was so sick was that I wasn't eating. I thought not eating was a good thing. Everyone was telling me how great and "healthy" I looked.

I never got more compliments from others than when I was starving myself.

But I was not healthy. I was just thinner. Healthy and thin are not the same thing.

I want to go back to the part of my story where I said that I believed that all my dreams could come true if I could just stop eating. Have you ever felt that way? I didn't get that idea from nowhere. From all around me, I was getting messages about *how* women are supposed to eat. I grew up

> Healthy and thin are not the same thing.

watching the women in my family try to eat as little as possible. I had been taught to never ask for seconds. I almost never saw women eating in movies or on shows. Whenever they did eat, it was always a vegetable and there was very little of it. When the women went on dates with men, the men ate amazing plates full of food and their dates ate salads.

What is up with a culture that thinks it's okay for women to be hungry all the time?

One of the reasons that girls and women feel pressure to eat less food is because of sexism. Sexism says that it doesn't matter if a girl or woman is hungry or unhappy as long as she meets the culture's beauty standard. Beauty standards—if you remember from Chapter 1—dehumanize girls and women, reducing us to bodies instead of seeing us as full humans. When we normalize the idea that girls and women should eat as little food as possible, we are creating a culture that says it doesn't matter how we feel, it only matters how we *look*.

We live in a culture that teaches us to be terrified of food. We live in a culture that teaches us that it's okay and normal to eat less than you want and even to skip meals. But it's not normal or okay.

When we are afraid of food, we do weird things that aren't good for us. Think of how you feel when you're afraid. You get stressed out, you start to obsess, you worry what will happen if you have to face this thing, and you spend time trying to avoid it. But the thing is, you can't avoid food, because human beings need food in order to survive.

You do not need to be scared of food. Hunger is one of our most basic survival instincts. We need food in order to think, to make good decisions, to have energy to move around, and to be able to focus and have our best ideas. Our brain needs food. Our body needs food. Food is good, not bad.

You should never feel pressure to skip a meal. "Fasting" is not a good idea. It creates anxiety around food and can affect your ability to concentrate and do stuff you love.

And let's not forget that food is really super amazing and delicious. Some of my best memories are around food. I remember one of my favorite times of year as a kid was the day after Thanksgiving, when my grandparents would sit out in the kitchen with pounds of leftover turkey, corn flour, and salsa, making tamales. I loved seeing my grandfather's hands covered in the slick fat from the meat. I loved watching my grandmother wrap each tamale with the floppy corn husk, like a baby being tucked into a blanket. I loved eating tamales throughout December, all the way up to Christmas. We had tamales only this one time of year, and they symbolized the specialness of the holidays to me.

I remember the first time I ever ate crème brûlée. I don't remember where I was or even how old I was, but I remember how good it felt to take my little silver spoon and crack the burnt sugar layer that stood between me and the eggy, creamy goodness underneath—like the ice on top of a lake in winter.

I remember being on the coast of Portugal and having the best steak I'd ever had. They brought it out with bread and oil, some sardines and olives. The steak was so good that about halfway through, I put down my fork and knife and started eating with my hands. I wanted to feel the steak between my fingers, bringing it up to my mouth. It was so delicious that I wanted my whole body to be involved in the process of eating it.

Our culture normalizes the fear of food because we're taught that if we eat too much, we'll be fat and that's bad. But what if there was no such thing as having a bad body?

If we stop believing that fatness is bad, then we can stop being afraid of food. We actually all know how to eat right. We know what our bodies need. We know when we're hungry. We know what we like.

You're at a perfect point in your life right now to question the fear of food that is a part of our culture.

write About It

Write about your favorite food-related memory. Describe the scenery, who was around you, the smell, the taste, and the way you felt.

14

Take Every Hour You Spend Criticizing Your Body and Do Something Else That's Totally Amazing

Before I started seriously questioning fatphobia and diet culture, I used to think about how much I hated my body all day long.

I remember thinking things like: *I can't be fat and have acne. I'm so embarrassed by how my stomach looks when I sit down. If I could just stop eating, then that dude I'm obsessed with would like me back. Once I become smaller, I'll be able to go to the beach. I wish I had enough discipline to have an eating disorder. Why am I hungry all the time? My double chin looks bad in all my pictures. I hate the way my legs look in a dress. I hate that my hair isn't straight enough. Why aren't my eyes bigger? Why am I so ugly? I deserve to have people make fun of me. Why are my arms so big? Why is my butt so flat? Why aren't my boobs even? I hate my leg hair.*

It was like a playlist in my head that never stopped. Instead of songs, everything on the playlist was a critical thought. They'd play over and over. I never got tired of hearing them. I didn't have a different playlist. I didn't know there *was* a different playlist.

Whenever I had a spare minute, I'd be thinking about how much better my life would be if I were thin. Whenever I ate, I'd be thinking about how I should be eating less so I could look more like my classmate everyone had a crush on. Whenever I went shopping for clothes, I'd spend the whole time hating what I looked like in the mirror and feeling bad when things didn't fit. It was a constant source of frustration and anxiety.

I never sat down with a calculator to see how much time I spent hating and criticizing my body, but thinking back on it, I know I almost never went a full hour without thinking of this stuff at least five or six times. That means I spent at least two hours every single day criticizing what I looked like. It was probably more than that, to be honest, but let's leave it at two.

Hours add up. So, in my case, that meant I was spending fourteen hours per week, 61 hours per month, 728 hours per year. That's 30 days out of 365. That's almost a tenth of an entire year. That's *a lot* of time.

And yeah, that's a lot of time lost, but there's another layer on top of that lost time. When you're thinking about how much you suck all the time, it makes it really, really hard to do anything else that makes you feel good. If you don't think you're good enough, you are much less likely to invest in the stuff that matters to you—because *you* don't matter to you. You might let people treat you badly because you think that's what you deserve. You might be crushing on someone who's a terrible person because you think it's okay for people to be terrible to you. If you're actively working to look different, then you also might postpone important stuff because you want to wait until you have the "right" body.

Before I learned about radical body positivity, I used to think that my life wasn't worth living until I was thin. I wanted to do all kinds of stuff—like be an artist, wear weird clothes, write a book, wear a bathing suit, dance. But I didn't do it, because I didn't think it was worth doing unless I looked a certain way.

That's what self-criticism does. It doesn't just take actual hours from you. It takes away the opportunity to become the incredible, magical, amazing person you were meant to be.

If self-criticism is so bad, then why do so many people do it?

Because that's what our culture teaches us to do. We see examples of girls and women hating their bodies all the time, in movies, on shows, and on the internet. We see it in ads. We see our parents do it, our teachers, celebrities. Sometimes it's obvious criticism, like "I hate my butt." Sometimes it's hidden in "inspiration," like "I would look better if I were just a little more _____ or a little less _____."

Girls of color are often facing two impossible beauty standards: the culture-wide white standard and our community-specific standard. For a lot of people of color, the community standard is the Coke bottle shape—little in the middle, with bigger chest and hips. Depending on who your friends are and what your family promotes, you might feel more pressure to conform to one than the other. Because my grandma was obsessed with white people and me being a "real American," the white standard was the one I felt more pressure to meet—even though there were almost no white people around me.

How many times a day do you have a negative thought about your body? Like when you look in the mirror after you wash your hands in the bathroom and criticize what your hair or skin or face looks like?

Most girls and women in the United States report that they feel dissatisfied with their bodies. It depends on the study, but some think as many as 80 percent of girls and women don't like the way they look.

Let's say you spend one full minute per day criticizing your body or how you look. There are seven days in a week, so that's seven minutes per week. There are roughly four weeks per month, so that's twenty-eight minutes per month. There are fifty-two weeks in a year, so that's 364 minutes per year. About six hours. Let's say you're going to live for another sixty years. That's 360 hours, or fifteen days. Here's a list of things you could do in fifteen days:

- Drive across the United States a few times

- Learn basic coding (HTML)

- Learn basic photo editing

- Learn the basics of playing an instrument

- Learn how to sew and actually make an entire look

- Learn how to make bread and bake some for every person at your school

- Start writing a novel

- Learn how to paint

- Learn the basics of a new language

- Write everyone you know a note telling them how amazing they are

- Start a garden

- Learn how to give a tarot reading

Guess what? You don't need to criticize yourself, because you are totally fine. In fact, you're totally perfect.

The first step? Make a promise to yourself, right now, to stop criticizing yourself out loud. That'll save you some time. Take a week, and see how it feels to stop saying mean stuff to yourself. As you're changing how you talk, begin to ask yourself: What do I want to do? What do I care about?

Stop giving away your precious time and do it now.

write About It

Write about an experience of you or a friend engaging in self-criticism. Now imagine you did something radically body-positive instead. What would you have done? What might the outcome have been?

15

Find Your Allies

When I first started thinking about becoming a fat activist, I was in school to get my master's degree. I wanted to interview fat women of color about their lives for my final research project. When I went to tell my professor that this was what I wanted to do, she told me that it was a bad idea.

She said that no one really cared about researching fat people, and that I would be messing up my chances of getting a job later if I did it. I was really sad when she said this, but I believed her because she was older and smarter than me.

When my boyfriend heard what she said, though, he got super upset. He said that her opinion was fatphobic. He encouraged me to find a different professor to work with, and he said he would help me find one. He stood up for me when I didn't know how to stand up for myself. He helped me to be strong when I wanted to give in. He knew that encouraging me to pursue my dream project was the right thing to do, and he helped me do it. I was able to go on and build an entire career around my passion because he was my ally at the very beginning.

The first time I ever heard about allies was when we hit the World War II unit in my history class in high school. "Ally" was the word for the countries that were on the same side of the fight to stop the Nazis from taking over the world. Later, I heard this word when I decided to become an activist. "Ally" was the word for the white people who were helping me fight to end racism. It was the word for the thin people who were helping me fight to end fatphobia. "Ally" was the word for someone like me, who is cisgender, who fights to end transphobia.

When I encourage you to "find your allies," I'm encouraging you to find the people in your life who:

1. Genuinely want you to thrive and succeed

2. You trust

3. Do what they can to make sure you are safe and successful

I'm talking about the people who are in your corner—not just people who agree with everything you say or who you see all the time. I mean someone who believes in you, cares about what you want and don't want, challenges you when you need to be challenged, sees that you are a good person who is capable of amazing things, and helps you have a good relationship with your body.

An ally can be a classmate, neighbor, coach, family member, friend, or boo. But not all your classmates, neighbors, coaches, family members, friends, or boos are necessarily your allies. I've had plenty of friendships and romantic relationships with people who didn't want me to thrive and/or didn't make me feel safe.

An ally can be a close friend, like your BFF. An ally can also be someone who isn't exactly your friend but who you still trust, and who wants to help you thrive and be safe—like an amazing teacher.

For a long time, I didn't think a lot about the people around me. I just accepted that I had to be friends with whomever was close by—even if they were mean to me or I didn't especially like them. In fact, for a long time I don't think I ever even really asked myself whether I liked a certain person or not. I was too busy worrying about whether other people liked me. I think I felt lucky that anyone wanted to hang around me because I was The Fat Girl and believed that I was an embarrassment. Or maybe I felt like I shouldn't complain, because I'd been taught that it is rude not to be nice to everybody and try to like everyone.

At that time, my community was made up of a lot of people who actually weren't that awesome. There was my family, who I loved a lot but who were also super messy and traumatizing. There were always fights at home. I remember always worrying about what was going to happen next—was everyone going to be laughing and cracking jokes at dinner, or was someone going to randomly upset my grandfather for no real reason and he would give everyone the silent treatment for five hours? Was my grandmother going to insult me because of my weight? I never knew when my mom was going to be in a bad mood. My brother didn't deal well with what was going on at home and would refuse to go to school sometimes. This really stressed me out because I wanted him to succeed and get out of the house. My aunt was sexually inappropriate with me, but no one seemed to notice her constantly "tickling" me or making weird, perverted jokes. Sure, they loved me and probably wanted me to succeed, but I didn't trust them and they didn't make me feel safe.

There was church, which I liked a little because it got me out of the house. Overall, though, church was hard because I was one of the only people of color and one of the only fat people in my youth group. Even though I tried really hard to get along with the other people my age, it never seemed to work out. I remember going to a sleepover with the girls my age and being the only fat girl. One of them put soy sauce in my hair and eyebrows while I was sleeping, and when I was too afraid to take a shower because I was scared they'd walk in on me and laugh. Then they made fun of me for being dirty.

I'll be honest: I think I also wasn't into church because I had problems with being told that all people are born bad, and that people could do really bad things and get away with them as long as they prayed before they died. I just didn't think that was true. So sure, the people at church helped me get out of my house, but I didn't trust them or think they cared about my success, and they didn't make me feel safe.

Then there were the people I went to school with. There were also lots of bullies at my school, and everyone acted like it didn't matter how mean they were. I was expected to forgive them and "be the bigger person." Always. I was expected to just accept that their behavior hurt me. Bullies are definitely not allies.

The only allies I felt really had my back were my closest friends. They really made life worth living.

When I was around them, those were the only times I really felt safe as a kid. We had our own weird jokes, and we had our own world. I felt lucky that I knew them, because they made me feel like I could do anything. Sometimes they didn't help me feel good about my body, but a good ally will always listen when you tell them that something is hurting you and when you set a boundary with them.

We live in a culture that teaches us that it's our job to just get along with everyone and pretend everything is fine even when it's not—especially if you're a girl.

But I think you deserve better. Even though we can't always control who is around us, we *can* control who we get close to. You have the power to choose whom you let into your VIP circle.

In order to figure out who your allies are (and how you can find more of them!), you've got to start by looking at all the people who are around you.

Let's start with where you live and hang out. Let's call this your "not chosen community (NCC)." Your NCC is made up of a lot of people—your family, your classmates, your teachers, your neighbors, the bus driver, the people who work at the grocery store you shop at, and anyone else who's around you, whether you like them or not. Maybe you wouldn't go to them if you had a personal problem, but they are still people you see and interact with. It's normal to have varying feelings about the people in your NCC. Those feelings might range from "This person is amazing" to "I would rather poke my eye out than hang out with them." You may be kinda forced to be around some of the people in your NCC: like maybe the bullies at your school or the person you don't really vibe with who's in your swimming class.

Most people get close to a few people in their NCC and then those people become chosen community (CC) or chosen family. Your CC is made up of your friends and mentors and the family members you connect with. These people are close to you: you feel like you can be yourself around them, you like and respect them, and you trust them.

The people closest to you should be your allies. You can help people become allies by teaching them what an ally is, if you want to—or you can just keep setting boundaries, and they can let you know once they're ready to become VIPs in your life.

Radical body positivity taught me that I deserve to be around people who want to see me thrive and who make me feel safe. When we thrive and feel safe, we are taking care of our minds, hearts, and bodies.

I want to share a few examples of what my romantic relationships, friendships, and family relationships look like today.

When it comes to my romantic relationships, I date people who love and celebrate my body and who I can turn to when I'm feeling scared or sad. They remind me that everything is going to be okay. They get excited when I get an award or something special happens in my life. They tell me when I'm doing something amazing. They remind me how beautiful I am. Before bed, my partner turns to me and tells me every part of my body that is lovely: "You have a cute nose. You have beautiful eyes. You have a cute smile. You have cute cheeks. You have a cute belly." This makes me feel good. This makes me feel safe and embodied. He celebrates my fat body, which is important to me, and he celebrates who I am as a writer and a person, which is also important to me.

When it comes to my friendships, I am only interested in getting close to people who are honest, kind, and who inspire me. My friends check in when I'm sick or sad. They come over if I need help. They make me food or tea when I visit them. They give me compliments. And I do the same. I congratulate them when they've done something amazing at their job or their outfit is particularly on-point. They call me when they need to talk about hard stuff, and I know I can turn to them when I need help figuring out a problem in my life.

When it comes to my family, I have learned to set boundaries with them. Even though it has been hard and I felt really guilty at first, I realized that I needed them to change how they treated me, in order to be okay. I started saying no to some of the things they asked me to do, and I decided to stop interacting altogether with my aunt. I needed my grandmother to stop making me feel bad about my body. I needed my mother to admit that her actions have hurt me and to take steps to prevent the same hurt from happening again. Pretending that everything was fine wasn't helping me or them. Remember how I said that being an ally isn't just about agreeing with someone all the time or letting them do whatever they want? When someone is acting in a way that's harmful to you, it's your job to say no. Accepting someone's abusive behavior isn't an act of love.

I've learned a lot about allies over the years.

I've learned that there's a difference between the people who happen to be around me and the people I choose to get close to.

I've learned that I have the power to choose whom I trust.

I've learned that I have the power to say no.

I've learned that I have the power to surround myself with people I love and who care about me.

I've learned that I can set boundaries or refuse to engage with people who treat me poorly.

I've learned that I can build a community filled with allies— people who make me feel really good and really loved and really safe.

You deserve that too!

write About It

Think of one or two people in your life who are your allies. What do they do that makes you feel loved, celebrated, and safe? Think of one or two people in your life you need to set boundaries with. What is one thing you can do to protect yourself from them?

16

wear what you want!

I want to tell you about one of the worst fights I ever had. It was with one of my former boyfriends, and it started because of one of my favorite accessories—a yellow umbrella.

This boyfriend had a really stressful job, so we didn't get to do much on the weekends because he always had to be at work. About a year into our relationship, he texted me one day and said he'd gotten a weekend off and suggested that we go out of town to celebrate. We got tickets to go to Phoenix, Arizona—in July. Most people are trying to leave Phoenix in the middle of July because it is over 100 degrees every single day. The sun beats down on you so hard that it feels like a tiny oven is strapped to your face. Because Arizona is the only state where four deserts come together, there are pretty much no trees to shield you from the brutal solar rays. It was so hot that we walked out of the airport and I was pretty much immediately soaking wet with sweat.

A long time ago a friend taught me that when the weather is that intense, you've got to create your own shade. I had packed my favorite umbrella for the trip. It was the same color as a psychedelic canary, and it was covered in drawings of tiny pugs wearing cute little outfits.

This umbrella was loud and playful and kind of extra, just like me. I loved that umbrella, and so I took it out whenever I had a chance.

On the second day, we set out to go to this little music festival in a town called Tempe. When we got there, there was not a single patch of available shade to hide under. So I pulled out my umbrella as we navigated the crowds of people. I was super excited that I had packed portable shade. It was at least 10 degrees cooler under my cute umbrella, and I was also shielding my skin from ferocious sunbeams.

All of a sudden, I started hearing my boyfriend sigh loudly and click his tongue. I looked over and he was seriously looking at my umbrella like it was made of chicken farts. At first I figured he was just grumpy because it was so freaking hot and he was jelly that I'd been smart enough to bring something to shield myself from a heat that no human should be forced to face alone. I asked him if he wanted to join me in the delicious cool air under my umbrella. He said no. After a while, he was getting weirder, and it became obvious that something was up but he didn't want to talk about what it was.

When we got home that night, I turned to him and asked what had happened. And he told me that I had decided to pull out a bright umbrella, and this made us stand out in a way that made him feel uncomfortable. I told him about the shade, the coolness, and the skin cancer I was avoiding. All he had to say in his defense was that no one else had an umbrella and that meant I shouldn't either.

It didn't take long before both of us were crying. I was so hurt that he thought I shouldn't do something because of what other people thought of me—especially because almost everyone at the festival was white. I also felt angry because I've spent my whole life being told that I should try to hide my body and hide myself, and I expected my boyfriend to stand up for me and understand how much it meant to be able to express myself. I expected him to understand how hard I had fought to be the kind of woman who was comfortable standing out, with an accessory that she loved. My boyfriend was wrong. It was not okay that he asked me to sacrifice something that mattered to me in order to help him conform.

When I got home and told my friend Nikki (who's also a woman of color) about what had happened, she pointed out something I hadn't thought about. She told me that because my boyfriend was a straight white dude, he was able to feel comfortable in most places because we live in a culture that was built to make him feel comfortable. I, on the other hand, do not feel comfortable in many places, because we live in a culture that wasn't built to make me feel comfortable.

He was afraid of my yellow umbrella because it made him feel like an outsider. I'm used to feeling like an outsider—whether I have a bright umbrella covered in dogs open or not.

That fight taught me a lot about why it's so important to wear what I want.

It's not my job to make other people feel comfortable. It's my job to be myself and wear what makes me feel good. It's my job to wear what I want.

What we wear tells a lot about our opinions, our gender expression, where we come from, and who we want to be in community with. Clothes are a form of silent communication. Many marginalized communities use clothing to show who they are so that others in that community will see them. Kind of like a secret code. For instance, I wear clothes that share a message: "I love my fat body. I am not trying to hide it." My bright, tight outfits are like a secret code that I'm sending to other people who are down to disrupt the cultural messaging around bodies.

Have you ever seen something you really, *really* wanted to wear but decided there was no way you'd be able to wear it without someone else being weird about it? I have.

I used to believe that there was no way I would ever wear a tight dress or a miniskirt or something neon-yellow. Let me tell you a little about my favorite stuff in my closet now: a cheetah-print coat, a cherry-red business suit, mustard-yellow high heels, neon-green pants, about ten humongous hats, a jumpsuit covered in silver sequins, feather boas, lace bodysuits, and about twenty-six bikinis.

I never thought I'd be the kind of person who wore tight neon pants or a silver-sequined jumpsuit.

When I was in middle school and high school, everything in my closet was pretty much the same color. The most adventurous color in my wardrobe was dark blue. I was taught that I had to hide my body. So I wore clothes that were too big for me and clothes that made me blend in as much as possible. Guess what? It didn't stop people from making fun of me. It didn't stop people from hurting me.

I felt like I had to dress like that, but it made me feel sad. I used to dream of the day that I'd be able to wear something I thought was cute and not be made fun of. I used to buy clothes that were too small because I thought they would inspire me to lose weight. Sometimes it was hard to find clothes in my size, but even if I did find something I liked in my size, I didn't want to wear it, because I was embarrassed for people to know I wanted to wear something pink or feminine.

It's never okay for someone to make fun of or treat someone badly because of what they're wearing. (This does not mean it's okay for people to wear stuff that says super-mean, sexist, racist, or homophobic stuff, though!)

The problem with the idea that only certain people who look a certain way get to wear what they want is that this silences other people. Silencing people really hurts them. People have the right to express themselves however they want—no matter what they look like, whether they are big or small, disabled or able-bodied, queer or straight, and wherever they reside on the gender spectrum. A lot of people think that they will wear what they want to wear someday in the future—"later," when they look different or live in a different place or when they have a boo.

It is important to take into account that people take different risks when wearing what makes them feel seen. Trans women, for instance, experience physical violence at high rates for wearing things that are not considered appropriate for their gender assigned at birth. Fat people often get verbally harassed or stared at for wearing bolder clothes.

I sometimes choose more muted looks on days when I'm feeling vulnerable. When I know I'm going to be around my fellow weirdos, though, I choose an outfit that's extra. I have friends all over the size, gender, and ability spectrum who wear exactly what they want because they'd rather risk harassment than edit their style, or because suppressing their selfhood comes at too big of a cost to their mental health. Trust your gut as you experiment with what you wear.

I asked my friend Bayley Van, a queer black femme and lifelong goth, her thoughts on fashion, identity, and risk. She said, "Sometimes it's more dangerous to smother yourself than to be smothered by society. Don't let the circumstances of the world force you to hurt yourself. Wear what you need to feel sane." Safety aside, if you're holding off on wearing what you want because you are worried about how you will look in it, I want to encourage you to push yourself just a little. You can start small.

Maybe you start with that necklace you've been wanting to wear, and see how that feels. Then move on to that scarf or blue eyeliner or hat you've been dreaming about showing off. If you're not ready to wear it outside, then ask a friend or two to come over so you can wear these looks for each other. I usually save my most wild, artsy looks for when I'm hanging out with my friends. There's no shame in that.

Another fat activist named Marilyn Wann wrote an article in which she said that fashion is like an alphabet we use to tell a story about who we are. Everyone should have access to the whole alphabet, not just one or two letters. Imagine trying to write a story about yourself but you can only use the letters "b," "t," and "f." Real hard. But many of us are trying to do just that.

No matter what anyone tells you, you have the right to express yourself with your wardrobe, makeup, and accessories. Some people will think they are entitled to tell you how they feel about what you wear, but if they have a problem, it is exactly that—*their* problem. You can look back at Chapter 9 to figure out what you want to say to people, before they even approach you with their opinions.

When we suppress our self-expression, we create a world where everyone is expected to look and act the same. When we self-express, we create opportunities for others to join us in being their true selves. When we self-express, we help to build a world where it's safe for people to be who they really are. Though you should never wear something you don't want to wear, I'd like to encourage you to show off if you've been holding back.

We've been taught that standing out is a really bad thing because it draws attention to us. That fear of visibility has a lot to do with race, gender, sexuality, and—weirdly enough—some of the history we learned about at the beginning of this book. People have fought for decades for the right to wear what they want, because fashion is a sacred form of self-expression that makes people feel seen. Everyone deserves to be seen, right?

✏️ Write About It

Describe your dream outfit, from head to toe. What do you like about this look? Do you already have some of the items? Who or what stops you from wearing what you love?

Conclusion

Whoa! You finished this book, which had about as much information as a freshman college class. That's a pretty big deal. Claps and snaps to you.

Yes, your eyeballs might have gotten super tired looking at thousands of words (I can relate), but this is not an ordinary book. This is a guide that—in your hands—has the power to start a revolution.

I hope you've learned something new, have new vocabulary to describe the stuff that's happening around you (like the way racism affects how you think of your body, which you read about in Chapter 4), think of something differently (like how each culture creates its own idea of who is beautiful, which you read about in Chapter 1), see yourself with a little more adoration (remember that you are precious and valuable always, and if you forget you can reread Chapter 10), and can recognize that you have unique, amazing magic. I hope you've also learned that you have a ton of power to transform your life, the lives of others, and this culture, through critical thought (remember, always question the culture, like you learned in Chapter 2), dreaming big about new traditions (for your biological and chosen fam, which you read about in Chapter 7), and through tools like setting boundaries (Chapter 12) and choosing your allies (Chapter 15).

Remember, you can always go back and look at stuff if you need reminders or want to brush up on, like, the definition of diet culture.

In these pages I've shared the best information and tools I've learned in the ten-plus years I've been a feminist and fat activist. I'm very glad that I got to share them with you because they have totally, without a doubt, changed my life. My life is full of sparkly moments, people I love, amazing outfits, delicious food (that I'm not ashamed to eat), and a love for myself that I earned by learning all the stuff I just taught you.

This book doesn't end here.

Just like all social justice work, it can't just be about making life better for one person. Now you have tools that most people don't. You have tools that all people need. You have the ability to understand the culture and make major changes to it. These things make you powerful beyond belief, and it's your job now to share them with others, like I've shared them with you.

So, go forward, Self-love Revolutionary, and spread the good word.

Acknowledgments

I'd like to thank my amazing, amazing editor at New Harbinger, Jennye Garibaldi, who had a vision for this project, who bought me beer and boquerones and convinced me that this book was possible, who advocated for me and invited me into the publishing process in a way I've never experienced, and who has been a listener and collaborator throughout the process of completing this book. Thank you to everyone on the marketing team at New Harbinger, who helped make this work come together. I'd like to thank the co-founders of the Radical Monarchs, Anayvette Martinez and Marilyn Hollinquest. Their radical vision for a robust, honest, healing, and empowering political education for girls of color shook me and has changed my life. They were the first people I thought of and reached out to when I began writing the book. Thank you to my mother and grandmother, Maria Nelly Tovar and Esperanza Tovar, who taught me to love myself even though no one had ever taught them how. Thank you to Mel Gruver, an Indiana activist and friend, for talking me through the ideation for this book as I anxiously perused the aisles of Michaels craft store for hours and hours. Thank you, Isabel Foxen Duke, my best friend and psychic sister, whose work and integrity have touched everything I do, who always processes with me and never turns down the invitation to go on a long walk through San Francisco to figure things out. Thank you to Dr. Kjerstin Gruys, a phenomenal sociologist and friend. Without her generous invitation to use her apartment for a writing retreat, I'm not sure how this book would have been written. Thank you to Bayley Van, who helped me process thoughts over iced Americano and princess cake. Thank you to my partner, Andrew, who made beef stroganoff while I edited and wrote way past bedtime, and who laid in bed or on the couch with me while I read him thousands of words, just to make sure I'd said exactly what I needed to say in exactly the way I needed to say it. Thank you for reminding me that I am beautiful, strong, and good, all the time. Thank you to the young women I spoke with at Wallenberg Traditional High School in San Francisco, whose astute analysis and honest observations about how race and gender shape their lives deeply informed this book. Thank you to the writers, educators, scholars, culture makers, and activists (and activist-scholars) who have helped teach me the tools that I share in this book—among them Donna K. Bivens, Michelle Tea, James Baldwin, Charlotte Cooper, Audre Lorde, Gloria Lucas, Marilyn Wann, Shooglet, Glenn Marla, Rebecca Popenoe, Sander Gilman, and Linda Bacon.

Endnotes

Chapter 1

1.   Abigail Haworth, "Forced to Be Fat," *Marie Claire*, June 21, 2011, www.marieclaire.com/politics/news/a3513/forcefeeding-in -mauritania/ (accessed October 24, 2019).

Chapter 3

2.   Y. Zafar, Joleen Hubbard, Eric Van Cutsem, F. Hermann, A. J. Storm, E. Gomez, C. Revil, and Axel Grothey, "Survival Outcomes According to Body Mass Index (BMI): Results from a Pooled Analysis of Five Observational or Phase IV Studies of Bevacizumab in Metastatic Colorectal Cancer (mCRC)," *Annals of Oncology* 26 (2015) (Suppl 4): vi117–iv121.

3.   National Association of Anorexia Nervosa and Associated Disorders, "Eating Disorder Statistics," ANAD.org, https://anad.org/ education-and-awareness/about-eating-disorders/eating-disorders- statistics/ (accessed October 24, 2019).

4.   Stuart Wolpert, "Dieting Does Not Work, UCLA Researchers Report," April 3, 2007, UCLA.edu, http://newsroom .ucla.edu/releases/Dieting-Does-Not-Work-UCLA-Researchers-7832 (accessed October 24, 2019).

5.   Ilan H. Meyer, "Prejudice, Social Stress, and Mental Health in Lesbian, Gay, and Bisexual Populations: Conceptual Issues and Research Evidence," *Psychological Bulletin* Vol. 129 (5) (2003): 674–697.

Chapter 4

6.   Coco Khan, "Skin-Lightening Creams Are Dangerous—Yet Business Is Booming. Can the Trade Be Stopped?" *The Guardian,* April 23, 2018, www.theguardian.com/world/2018/apr/23/skin -lightening-creams-are-dangerous-yet-business-is-booming-can -the-trade-be-stopped (accessed January 3, 2019).

7.   Derald Wing Sue, "Microaggressions: More Than Just Race," *Psychology Today,* November 17, 2010, www.psychologytoday.com /us/blog/microaggressions-in-everyday-life/201011/microaggressions -more-just-race (accessed January 3, 2019).

8.   Carson Kessler, "How Three Asian Women Dealt with Their Eyelid Insecurities," Vice.com, June 13, 2018, https://tonic.vice.com /en_us/article/qvnnjd/how-three-asian-women-dealt-with-their -eyelid-insecurities (accessed January 3, 2019).

9.   Viola Zhou, "Why Double Eyelid Surgery Is on the Rise in Asia: Rising Incomes and Acceptance, and Star Power of Fan Bingbing, Angelababy," *South China Morning Post,* May 15, 2017, www.scmp.com/lifestyle/health-beauty/article/2093921/why -double-eyelid-surgery-rise-asia-rising-incomes-and (accessed January 3, 2019).

10.   Ibid.

11.   The Annie E. Casey Foundation, "New Study: The 'Adultification' of Black Girls," July 26, 2017, www.aecf.org/blog/new-study-the-adultification-of-black-girls/ (accessed January 3, 2019).

Chapter 5

12.   Chia-Yu Chang, Der-Shin Ke, and Jen-Yin Chen, "Essential Fatty Acids and Human Brain," *Acta Neurologica Taiwanica* 18(4) (2009): 231–41.

13.   Ibid.

14.   Albert J. Stunkard, Terryl T. Foch, Zdenek Hrubec, "A Twin Study of Human Obesity," *Journal of the American Medical Association* 256(1) (1986): 51–54.

15.   Gilder Lehrman Institute of American History, "Sylvester Graham and Antebellum Diet Reform," http://ap.gilderlehrman.org/history-by-era/first-age-reform/essays/sylvester-graham-and-antebellum-diet-reform (accessed January 3, 2019).

16.   Matt Soniak, "Corn Flakes Were Part of an Anti-Masturbation Crusade," MentalFloss.com, March 7, 2018, https://mentalfloss.com/article/32042/corn-flakes-were-invented-part-anti-masturbation-crusade (accessed January 3, 2019).

17.   Donald L. Fixico, "When Native Americans Were Slaughtered in the Name of 'Civilization,'" The History Channel, March 2, 2018, www.history.com/news/native-americans-genocide-united-states (accessed January 3, 2019).

Chapter 6

18.   Kelsey Miller, "Study: Most Girls Start Dieting by Age 8," Refinery29.com, January 26, 2015, www.refinery29.com/en-us /2015/01/81288/children-dieting-body-image (accessed November 12, 2018).

Chapter 10

19.   David Garner, "Body Image in America: Survey Results," *Psychology Today*, https://www.psychologytoday.com/us/ articles/199702/body-image-in-america-survey-results (accessed January 2, 2019).

20.   Catherine M. Shisslak, Marjorie Crago, and Linda S. Estes, "The Spectrum of Eating Disorders," *International Journal of Eating Disorders* Vol. 18 (1995): 209-219.

Chapter 12

21.   Arlie Hochschild and Anne Machung, *The Second Shift* (New York: Penguin Books, 2003).

Virgie Tovar, MA, is one of the nation's leading experts and lecturers on fat discrimination and body image. She holds a master's degree in sexuality studies with a focus on the intersections of body size, race, and gender. She is the founder of Babecamp, a four-week online course designed to help people who are ready to break up with diet culture, and creator of the hashtag campaign #LoseHateNotWeight. Tovar edited the anthology, *Hot & Heavy: Fierce Fat Girls on Life, Love and Fashion;* and is author of *You Have the Right to Remain Fat,* which was placed on the American Library Association's Amelia Bloomer List. She is a contributor for *ForbesWomen* and *Bedsider,* and was named one of the top fifty most influential feminists by *Bitch Magazine.* She is a recipient of the Poynter Fellowship in Journalism at Yale University. Tovar has been featured in *The New York Times* and *Tech Insider,* and on MTV, Al Jazeera, and Yahoo Health. She lives in San Francisco, CA.

More Instant Help Books for Teens